Tarot Café

THE COLLECTOR'S EDITION: BOOK 2

SANG-SUN PARK

This collector's edition book combines volume 3 - 6 of the *Tarot Café* original publication.

Story So Far...

A sultan who has fallen in love with a young slave... A poor student who drives away a lake fairy over doubt and jealousy... A dragon that seeks to avenge the death of a dear friend... These are just a few of the supernatural beings that Pamela, owner of The Tarot Café, has welcomed through the doors of her mysterious establishment. But can she help them while dealing with a deep, dark secret of her own?

Pamela

Table of Contents

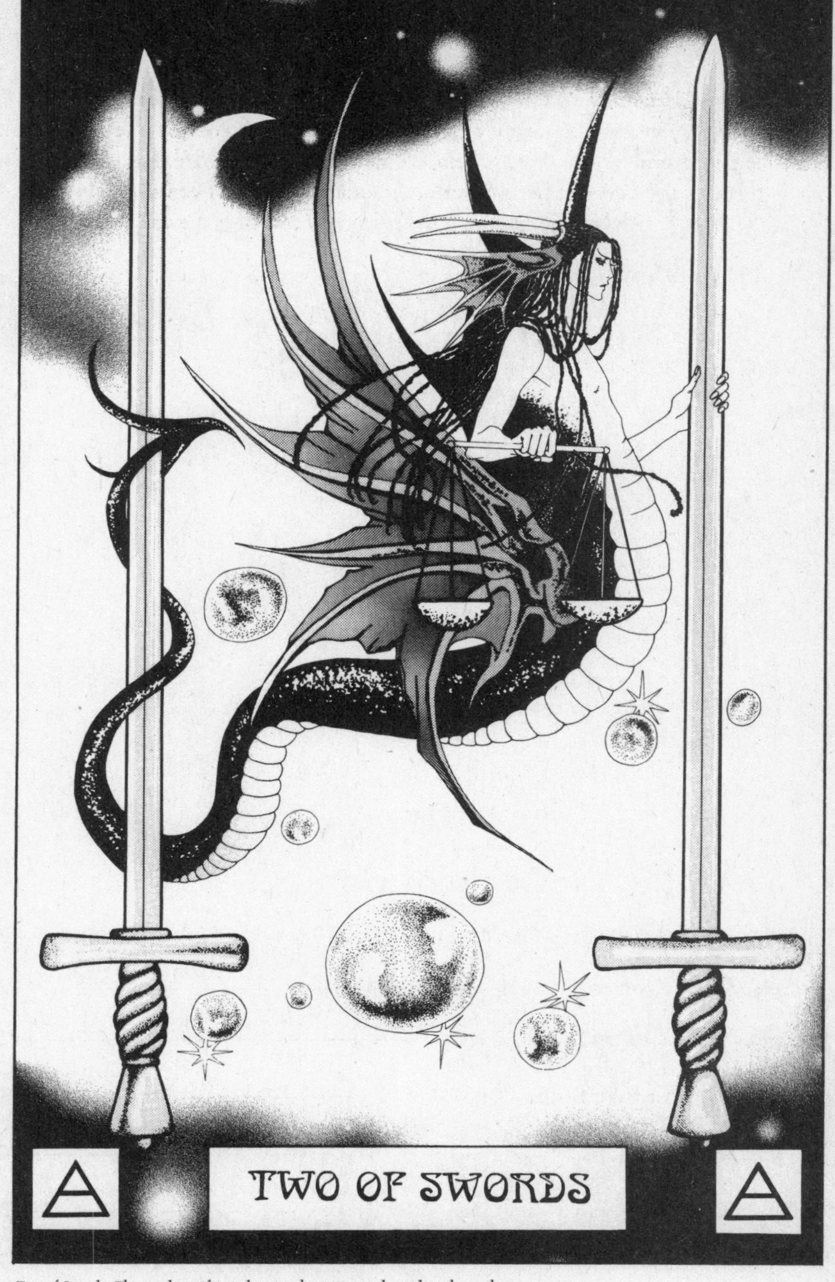

ILLUSTRATION FROM THE DRAGON TAROT

*Two of Swords: This card signifies indecision, hesitation and avoiding the truth.

SO YOU'RE SAYING THAT I'M A DRAGON...
...AND YOUR LONG-LOST FRIEND?
YES, THAT'S RIGHT.
IS BELUS BEHIND ALL THIS? IS HE PLAYING A TRICK ON ME?
YOU MEAN YOU DON'T REMEMBER ANYTHING?

THERE'S NOTHING TO REMEMBER!

IF I REALLY WERE A DRAGON, I'D BREAK THIS CHAIN, BEAT YOU UP AND GET THE HELL OUT OF HERE.

I DON'T HAVE WINGS.

I CAN'T BREATHE FIRE.

THAT' BECAUSE YOU'VE LOST YOUR DRAGON HEART TO THAT WOMAN.

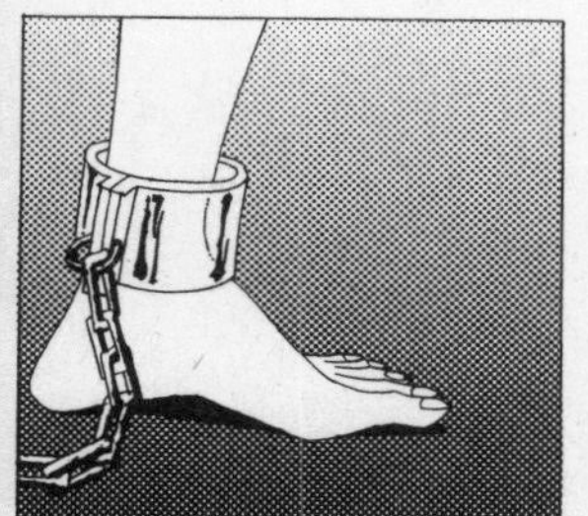

AND THAT CHAIN IS MADE OF ORIHALCON.* EVEN A DRAGON CAN'T BREAK IT EASILY.

*Orihalcon is mythical metal of extreme strength.

MY DRAGON HEART?
TO PUT IT SIMPLY, A DRAGON'S HEART IS WHAT GIVES IT ITS POWER.
IN MY CASE, IT GIVES ME THE POWER TO CONTROL THUNDER AND WIND.

SO PAMELA KILLED HIM AND TOOK HIS HEART?

SHE DIDN'T STRIKE ME AS A BAD PERSON, THOUGH.

NEVER, NEVER AGAIN!

DON'T SAY HER NAME IN FRONT OF ME!

SORRY. I LOSE CONTROL WHENEVER I HEAR HER NAME.

IN ANY CASE, I'M GLAD THAT YOU'RE ALIVE.

칫

I WAS THE ONE WHO STAGED THE KIDNAPPING BEFORE, BUT WHAT SHOULD I DO NOW? HOW CAN I GET OUT OF HERE?
HMM...YOU LOOK YOUNGER THAN YOU USED TO.
ALECTO.
DO YOU LIKE ME?

WHAT ARE YOU TALKING ABOUT?
BAM
AAACH!
GET SOME SLEEP! YOU'LL BE STAYING HERE FOR A WHILE.
I GUESS HYPNOSIS DOESN'T WORK ON A DRAGON.
OH, THAT WAS CLOSE...
두근 두근 두근

*High Priestess: This card represents the feminine element in a relationship; the ideal mother or wife who gives strength to loved ones. It may also indicate mystery, wisdom and hidden influence.

I GUESS I HAVE NO CHOICE BUT TO FIND THE ANSWER WITHIN MYSELF... I'LL HAVE TO TALK TO ALECTO.

딸칵
PAMELA, I CALLED THE NUMBER ASH GAVE ME...
...BUT I CAN'T GET THROUGH.

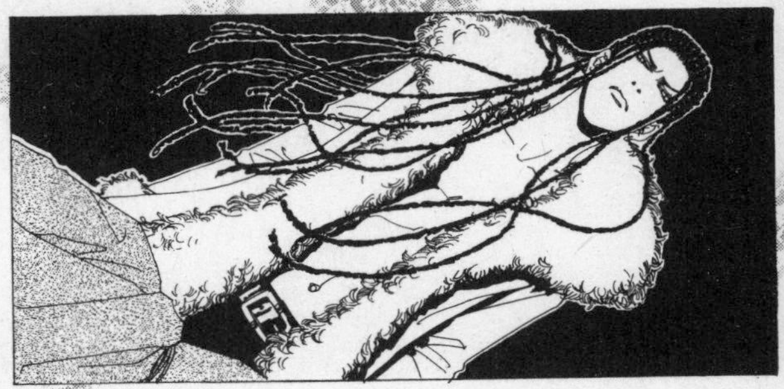

YOU LEAVE ME IN CHAINS AND CREEP INTO MY BED AT NIGHT? ISN'T THAT A LITTLE WEIRD?

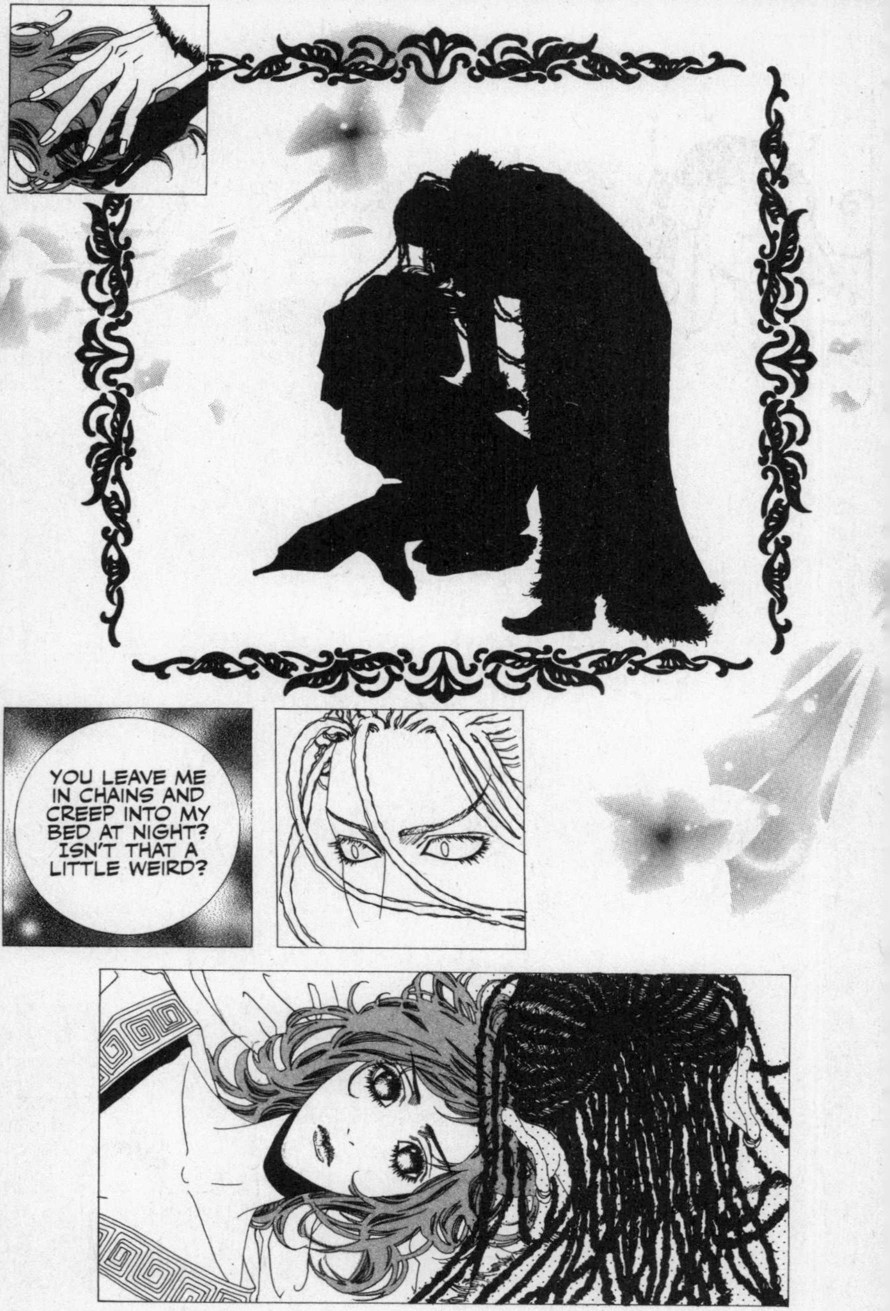

I-I DIDN'T...
흠...

I WASN'T TRYING TO DO ANYTHING...

HMM, HE'S CUTER THAN I THOUGHT. I BET A DRAGON CAN MAKE A PRETTY GOOD PET.

IF YOU UNCHAIN ME, I'LL BELIEVE YOU.

FOR THE FIRST 100 YEARS, I LOOKED FOR YOU AND PAMELA, AND THEN I FELL ASLEEP...

AND THEN JUST RECENTLY I HEARD THAT PAMELA WAS SEEN SOMEWHERE...

SO YOU SPENT ALL THESE YEARS LOOKING FOR HIM, HUH?

YOU POOR THING... YOU MUST HAVE BEEN VERY LONELY.

WELL...NOT REALLY.

HOW CAN YOU BE SO SURE THAT I'M ASH AFTER ALL THIS TIME?

DO YOU EVEN REMEMBER HIS FACE?

WITHOUT A DOUBT!
I WOULD RECOGNIZE YOU EVEN IF YOU LOOKED DIFFERENT.
불끈

HEH...I GUESS WE WERE REALLY CLOSE, HUH?
I'M SORRY THAT I CAN'T REMEMBER.

TO TELL YOU THE TRUTH...
YOU MUST HAVE HATED ME...I DIDN'T TREAT YOU VERY WELL.

HE'S REALLY CUTE! HE HAD AN ATTITUDE BEFORE...
BUT NOW HE SEEMS STUPID AND NAIVE...JUST THE WAY I LIKE IT!

NO, I DON'T THINK SO! I MUST HAVE LIKED YOU A LOT, ALECTO.
THAT'S RIGHT!
YOU MIGHT REMEMBER SOMETHING IF I SHOWED YOU THE WAY YOU USED TO LOOK.
I, THE BLACK KING, BID YOU...
NOEADEN*, SHOW YOUR-SELF!

*Noeaden: Spirit of the earth

AMAZING!
AMAZING?!

THIS IS THE DRAGON ASH? HE LOOKS JUST LIKE ME!

...DO YOU REMEMBER YOUR FULL NAME?

FULL NAME? WHAT DO YOU MEAN?

OUR NAMES ARE A CONTRACT WITH THE GODS AND CARRY THEIR OWN POWER.
SO YOU MUST REMEMBER NEVER TO SPEAK YOUR NAME LIGHT-HEARTEDLY.

ALL RIGHT...

ASHES KAYOMART DI AKRASIEL TIAMAT.

ASH?

주춤!

THAT'S YOUR NAME.

IT HURTS!
IT FEELS LIKE MY HEART IS BEING RIPPED FROM MY CHEST!

ASH? STAY AWAKE! ASH!

WHAT'S HAPPENING TO HIM? HE ONLY HEARD HIS OWN NAME...

YOU...YOU ARE!!

IT'S BEEN A WHILE, ALECTO. IT'S BEEN SO LONG THAT I CAN BARELY REMEMBER YOU.

BERIAL! WHAT ARE YOU DOING?!

WELL, IT'S RUDE TO MESS WITH SOMEONE ELSE'S GAME PIECE. HA HA HA.

GAME? WHAT ARE YOU TALKING ABOUT?
WHAT'S HAPPENING? I FEEL POWERLESS.
YOU PATHETIC BEING...YOU DON'T BELONG TO THE LIGHT OR TO THE DARK. SLEEP WELL.

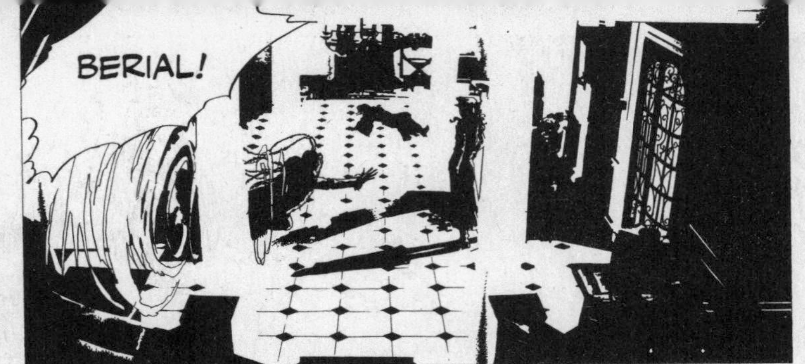

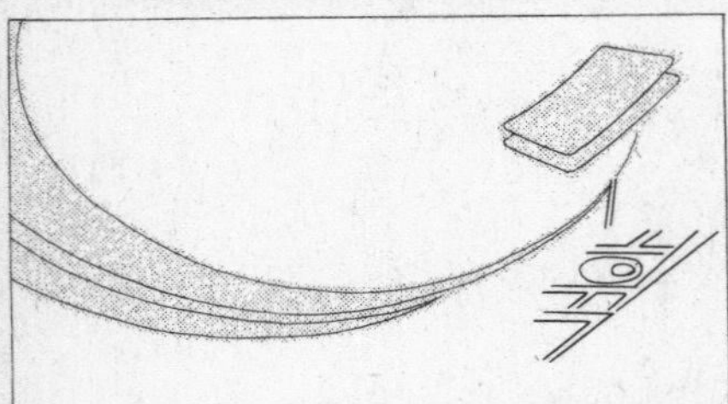

XV

XVIII

THE DEVIL

THE MOON

DEVIL?!

*The Devil: This card represents submission, destruction, malice, flattery, bad influence, black magic and unexpected failure.

*The Moon: This card represents deception, uncertainty, disillusionment, danger and negative influences.

IS HE THE ONE CORA WAS TALKING ABOUT? THE ONE HIDING BEHIND THE MOON?
ASH!

XVII The Stars

Episode 11:
A Butterfly in
My Dreams

Le Stelle
Les Étoiles

Der Stern
La Estrella

The Stars: This card represents inspiration, a feeling of wanting to give back, hope at the end of the tunnel, and serenity during times of upheaval.

ILLUSTRATION FROM FEY TAROT

NEED SOME HELP?
...?
FIND A WOMAN NAMED PAMELA.
SHE'LL TELL YOU EVERYTHING YOU WANT TO KNOW.

A VACATION IN A QUIET PLACE UNTIL THE REPAIRS ON THE CAFE ARE FINISHED...I GUESS IT'S A NICE ENOUGH PLACE.
I WISH BELUS HADN'T DECIDED TO TAG ALONG.
YOU'RE ALWAYS SO TOUCHY AROUND BELUS, PAMELA.
YOU SAY YOU HAVE A "CONTRACTUAL RELATIONSHIP" WITH HIM, BUT I WONDER IF YOU REALLY LIKE HIM.
DIDN'T I TELL OU I'D SELL YOU O THE BUTCHER IF YOU SAID THAT AGAIN?
AAAH! I'M SORRY, I'M SORRY!
WELL, THEN, I'M GOING OUT TO MEET BELUS.
SHE'S JUST BEING A CRAZY OLD SPINSTER. I'M OUTTA HERE BEFORE SHE EXPLODES.

멈칫

ASH... WHAT IF SOMETHING HAPPENED TO HIM?

I CAN'T GET IN TOUCH WITH HIM AFTER WHAT HAPPENED THAT DAY.

AH...I GUESS IT'S GOTTEN WARMER.

A BUTTERFLY...

MY...MY EYELIDS ARE
SO HEAVY...

ARE YOU PAMELA?

SOMEONE TOLD ME TO FIND YOU.
I CAME TO ASK YOU SOMETHING.

Six of Swords: Right-side up, this card signifies a trip overseas, a gesture toward reconciliation, possibly with the help of another person. Upside down, it represents a dilemma with no immediate solution.

THERE IS SOMEONE YOU WANT TO RECONCILE WITH BEFORE YOU LEAVE ON A LONG JOURNEY.

THAT'S WHY YOU CAME TO ME?

FAY WAS SEVEN YEARS OLD WHEN WE FIRST MET...

SHE LOOKED LIKE A DOLL, STANDING THERE HOLDING A MUSIC BOX LEFT TO HER BY HER MOTHER.
THEY SAID FAY WAS MY SISTER. SHE CAME TO LIVE WITH US WHEN HER MOTHER DIED.

YOUR MOTHER WAS NOTHING BUT A WHORE. I'VE DECIDED TO ACCEPT YOU OUT OF KINDNESS, BUT...

OF COURSE, THERE'S NO CERTAINTY THAT YOU'RE REALLY MY CHILD.

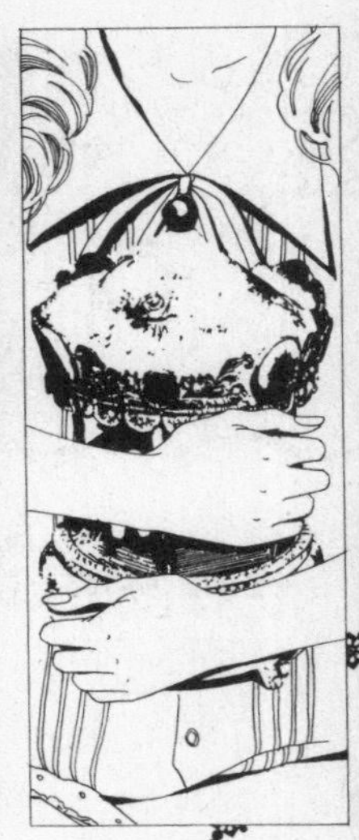

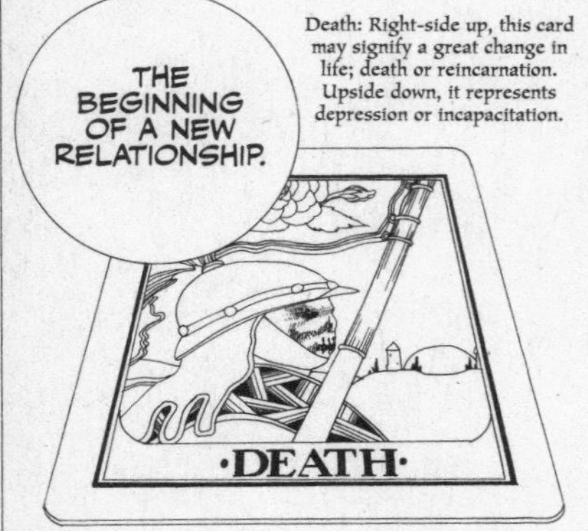
THE BEGINNING OF A NEW RELATIONSHIP.
Death: Right-side up, this card may signify a great change in life; death or reincarnation. Upside down, it represents depression or incapacitation.
·DEATH·

AND A SUDDEN DEATH...

YES, MY FATHER DIED.

SOME SAID THAT FAY'S MOTHER DIED THE SAME WAY.

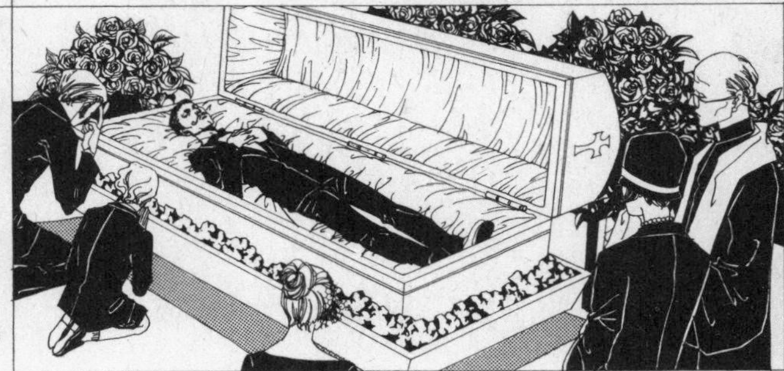

MY MOTHER HATED FAY. SHE HAD HER LOCKED UP IN THE ATTIC TO LIVE IN ISOLATION, LIKE A LEPER.

버둥
버둥

YOU FILTHY LITTLE THING!
HERE, EAT THIS!

퐁당
우적
우적

EAT!

HA HA HA! YOU LIKE IT? THAT'S THE STUFF WE FEED TO PIGS!

아구 아구
꾸욱
DO YOU KNOW WHAT PEOPLE ARE SAYING?
THAT YOU'RE NOT MY FATHER'S CHILD. YOU'RE THE *DEVIL'S* CHILD.
스윽..

두근 두근
PERHAPS IT WASN'T ALL LIES. FAY REALLY WAS DIFFERENT FROM US. THE WAY SHE LOOKED, BEHAVED...

THE STRANGE THING WAS THAT I DREAMT OF FAY OFTEN. IN MY DREAMS, SHE WOULD LOOK DOWN ON ME, SMILING.
EVEN THOUGH IT WAS ONLY A DREAM, IT FELT GOOD TO SEE HER SMILING LIKE THAT.

THERE WAS A SPRING DAY, WHEN FAY WAS THIRTEEN AND I WAS FIFTEEN.

AROUND THAT TIME OF YEAR, BUTTERFLIES WOULD COME SEARCHING FOR THEIR MATES.

YOU'VE NEVER SEEN IT, RIGHT? I'VE SEEN IT HUNDREDS OF TIMES.
YOU WANNA GO SEE?

WELL, GET MOVING.
SHAKE SHAKE
CAN YOU WORRY WHEN YOU'RE ESTING?

CREEP CREEP
AAAAAH!
BAM!!

YOU THINK...
...THIS IS FUNNY?

THAT'S WHAT YOU GET FOR LAUGHING AT ME!

THIS IS A MALE APATURA IRIS. IT GLOWS A FAINT PURPLE AT NIGHT.

SHANDY!
SHANDY! WHERE ARE YOU?

IT'S MY MOTHER!

DON'T TOUCH THAT! IF YOU BREAK IT, I'LL KILL YOU!

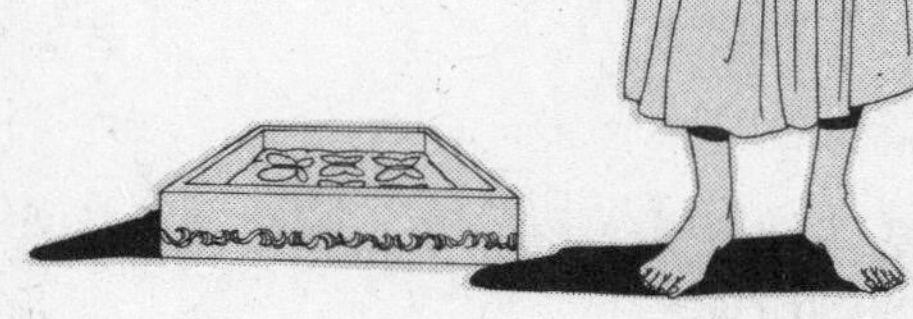

SHE BAKED A STRAWBERRY CAKE. I BROUGHT SOME FOR YOU.
YOU STUPID IDIOT!
DO YOU KNOW HOW HARD IT IS TO CATCH ONE OF THOSE THINGS?

B-
BLOOD!

FAY...

WAAAAAH!!

I SHOULDN'T HAVE DONE THAT...

Five of Rods: Right-side up, this card represents a fierce struggle to acquire material wealth as well as validation from other people. It may also signify competition and rivalry. Upside down, it may signify deception or legal problems.
FIVE OF RODS

AFTER THAT, SHE WAS AFRAID OF ME AS WELL.
YOU WERE BLINDED BY TRIVIAL ISSUES AND FAILED TO SEE WHAT WAS REALLY IMPORTANT.

AFRAID OF YOU AS WELL? WHAT DO YOU MEAN BY THAT?

Eight of Swords: This card may represent difficulty, imprisonment, danger, futile hopes, or needing guidance and clarity.

FAY WAS AFRAID OF PEOPLE...OR MAYBE PEOPLE WERE JUST AFRAID OF FAY.

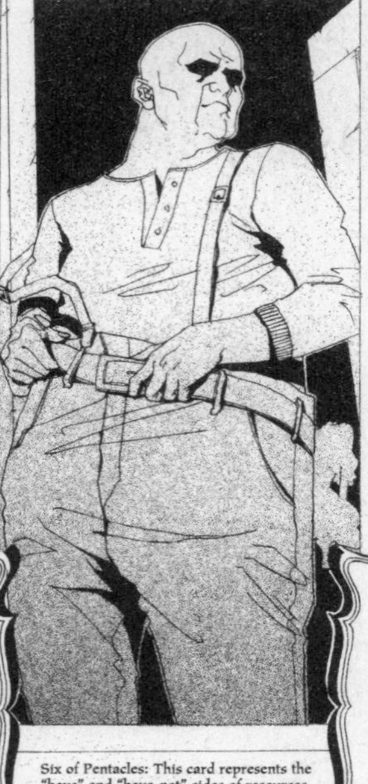

I DON'T KNOW WHAT THEY DID TO HER, BUT ONCE IN A WHILE, I WOULD HEAR HER SCREAM.

Six of Pentacles: This card represents the "have" and "have-not" sides of resources, knowledge and power. It signifies the huge middle ground where it is not exactly clear who has what.

SIX OF PENTACLES
SO YOU WANTED TO MAKE UP FOR HITTING HER?
TO PROVE THAT YOU WERE DIFFERENT FROM THEM?

THAT'S NOT IMPORTANT, IS IT?

WHY?
I GUESS IT HURT YOUR PRIDE TO REVEAL YOUR HEART TO A ROOTLESS BEGGAR OF A GIRL, HUH?

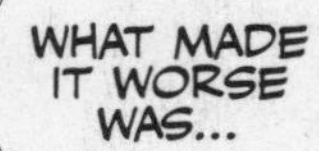

Wheel of Fortune: This card represents an unexpected turn in life or the beginning of good karma; changing the consequences of past events. It may also signify bad fortune or an unwanted turn of events.

AAAAH!

SHANDY!!

SINCE THAT GIRL CAME INTO THEIR HOUSE, THEY'VE SEEN SO MUCH MISFORTUNE...
HOW SAD... HE WAS ONLY FIFTEEN.
HE DROWNED IN THE WELL, HUH? SHE PROBABLY PUT A CURSE ON HIM.

MOTHER THOUGHT FAY WAS RESPONSIBLE FOR MY DEATH, SO...

찰싹 — 찰싹
찰싹 — 찰싹
찰싹 찰싹
스으으으

IT WON'T BE THAT EASY.
TRYING TO KILL ME, ARE YOU?

AFTER SHE DIED, ALL THE SERVANTS LEFT THE HOUSE AND LITTLE FAY WAS LEFT BEHIND. SHE LIVED ALL ALONE IN THAT EMPTY HOUSE.

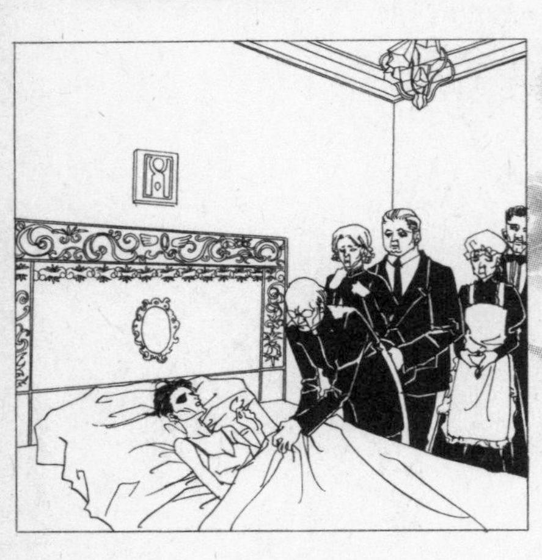

NO ONE WOULD GO NEAR HER.

SHE PROBABLY FELT VERY LONELY. BUT THE MORE ALONE SHE FELT, THE FARTHER PEOPLE DISTANCED THEMSELVES FROM HER.

ONE AFTER ANOTHER, PEOPLE DIED UNDER STRANGE, UNEXPLAINABLE CIRCUMSTANCES. MANY MORE LEFT, AND THE TOWN EVENTUALLY BECAME EMPTY.

NO MATTER HOW MANY BUTTERFLIES SHE COLLECTED, SHE WAS STILL ALONE.
SHE WAS SURROUNDED BY ALL THOSE MOUNTED BUTTERFLIES, BUT IN REALITY, SHE WAS THE ONE MOUNTED IN A BOX.

NO MATTER HOW MUCH YOU LOVE SOMEONE, IF YOU DON'T EXPRESS YOURSELF, THE OTHER PERSON WON'T KNOW HOW YOU FEEL.
XIX
THE SUN
The Sun: This card represents understanding, experiencing greatness and joy; forgiving yourself.

HOW CAN I HELP SET HER FREE?

TELL FAY HOW YOU FEEL ABOUT HER. THAT'S HOW YOU CAN SET FREE HER.

OKAY, I WILL.
AND THERE'S SOMETHING I WANT TO GIVE HER, TOO.

살랑

?
딩동
딩동
샤랑

I WANTED TO
GIVE YOU THIS.

GORGON

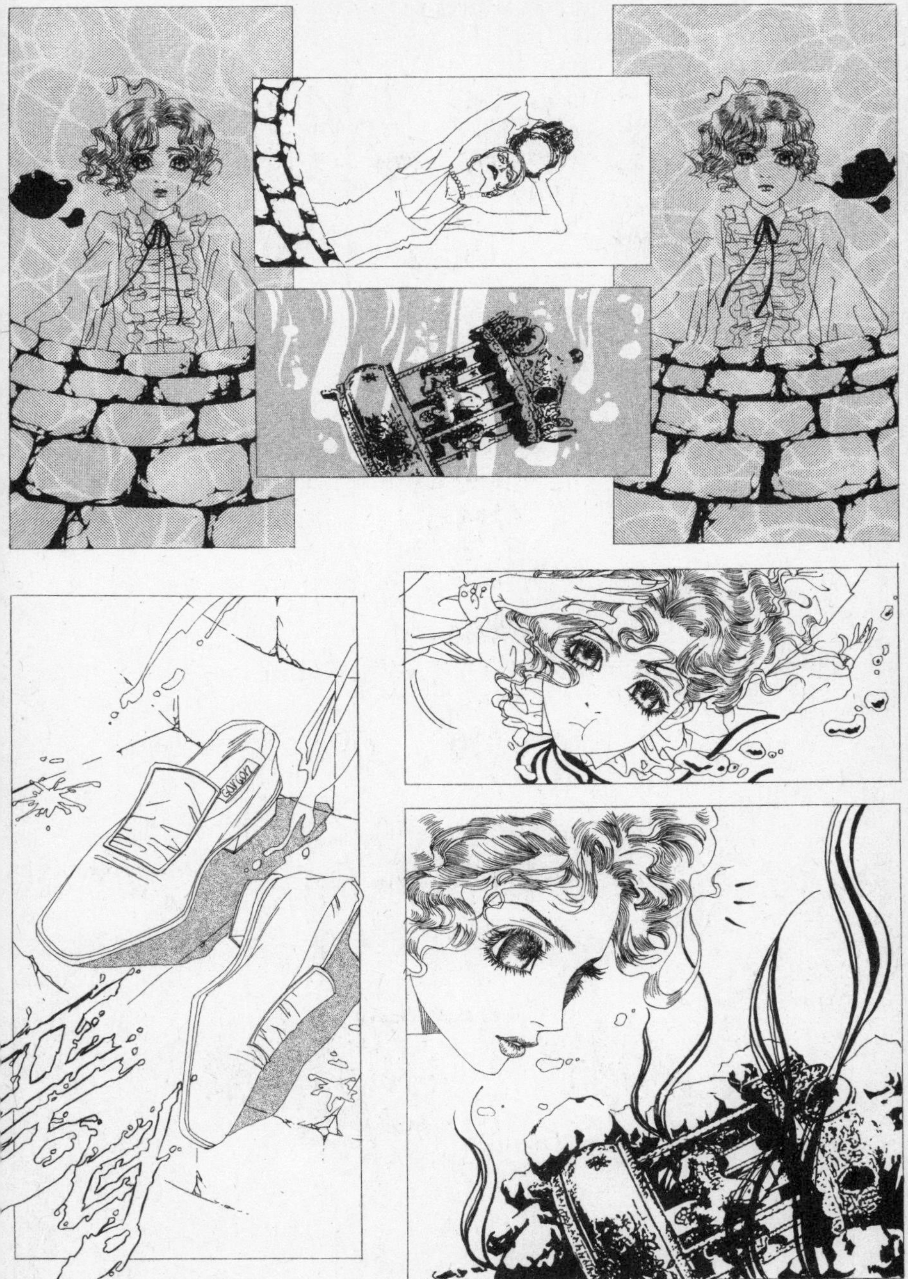

득
우득
......?

I COULDN'T SAY IT BECAUSE I FELT SO STUPID...

I LIKE YOU.
WILL YOU COME WITH ME?

...LA...
...MELA...
PAMELA!

THAT WAS A POWERFUL KISS! IT NEARLY BROKE MY TEETH.

WHAT THE HELL ARE YOU TRYING TO DO?!

WHAT AM I TRYING TO DO? YOU'RE TOO MUCH!

PAMELA, YOU SLEPT FOR THREE DAYS STRAIGHT.

I SLEPT FOR *THREE DAYS?* WHAT HAPPENED TO THE BOY?
WHAT BOY? ARE YOU TALKING IN YOUR SLEEP OR SOMETHING?

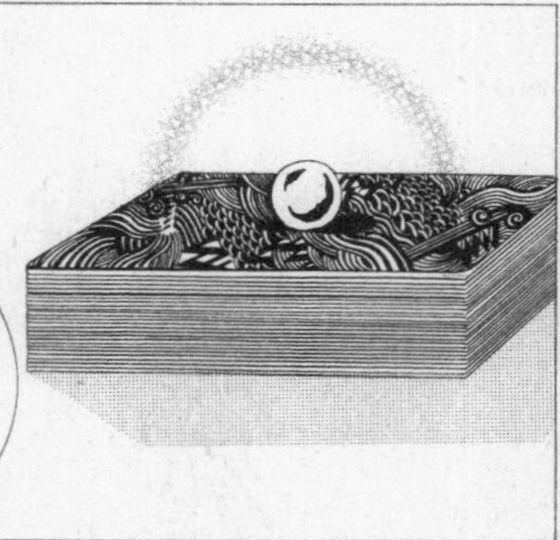

......

I HEAR NO ONE LIVES THERE ANYMORE.
SOME GIRL WAS BLAMED FOR THE PLAGUE THAT STRUCK THE TOWN. THE TOWNSPEOPLE LOCKED HER UP IN THAT MANSION UNTIL SHE DIED. ISN'T THAT HORRIBLE?

AH, I SEE...BUT EVERYTHING IS OKAY NOW.

TUNRIDHA, VOLVA: NORSEMEN BELIEVE THAT AN EVIL WITCH, TUNRIDHA, OR A SHAMAN, VOLVA, IS RESPONSIBLE FOR NIGHTMARES.

A WITCH'S SPIRIT TRAVELS OUT OF HER BODY AT NIGHT, THEY BELIEVE. THEN IT CAUSES DAMAGE TO YOUR HOUSE OR HARASSES YOU WHILE YOU SLEEP.

ARE YOU AWAKE?
AH...MY HEAD HURTS! WHAT HAPPENED?
YOU COLLAPSED IN FRONT OF MY HOUSE. YOU'VE BEEN SLEEPING FOR THREE DAYS...I DON'T KNOW EXACTLY WHAT HAPPENED TO YOU.
IF YOU NEED ANYTHING, LET ME KNOW.

ASH, YOU DON'T RECOGNIZE THAT MAN?
AAAAH...
콸콸

Episode 12: Contract

ILLUSTRATION FROM MASTER TAROT

Wachet
On watch

Wachet on Watch: The attitude of a traveler who leaves everything behind and embarks on a journey; a volatile situation; the need to be wary of sudden disasters or hardships.

BERIAL WAS "THE PRINCE OF DECEIT AND FALSEHOOD," A DEVIL "THAT HELD NOTHING SACRED."
HE HAD A NECKLACE WITH IMMENSE POWER.

BUT FOR SOME REASON, THE NECKLACE BROKE, AND THE BEADS FELL TO THE EARTH.
LIKE METAL TO A MAGNET, THE BEADS GRAVITATED TO PEOPLE WITH EXTRAORDINARY POWERS, WHO THEN BECAME THEIR NEW OWNERS.

THE BEADS GAIN POWER AND MEANING ONLY WHEN THEY COME TOGETHER IN A NECKLACE. SEPARATED, THEY REMAIN ORDINARY BEADS.
SEPARATED, THEY GIVE NO POWER TO THE PEOPLE WHO POSSESS THEM.
BUT, LIKE SO MANY THINGS IN THIS WORLD, THEY HAVE DIFFERENT MEANINGS DEPENDING ON THE PERSON WHO POSSESSES THEM.
FOR INSTANCE, TO ME, THOSE BEADS SIGNIFY THE END OF A LONG, BORING JOURNEY...

WORK IN PROGRESS

YOU THERE! WAIT!
I'VE BEEN WAITING FOR YOU FOR THREE DAYS!

I'VE BEEN WATCHING YOU FOR A LONG TIME.
HOW...HOW MUCH DO YOU WANT?

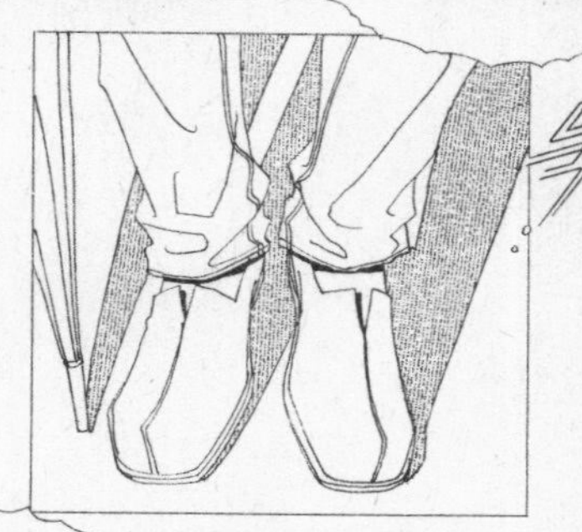

I...I ADORE YOU...
I DON'T KNOW HOW IT HAPPENED, BUT I FELL IN LOVE WITH YOU AT FIRST SIGHT!

I'M SORRY, BUT....

YOU'RE NOT EXACTLY MY TYPE.

......
IF I HAD MORE TIME, I MIGHT HAVE PLAYED WITH YOU A BIT, BUT AS IT HAPPENS, I'M EXTREMELY BUSY AT THE MOMENT.
CIAO!

철컥
WELL THEN, YOU LEAVE ME NO OTHER CHOICE.

YOU LIKE ME...
...THAT MUCH?

IN THAT CASE...

I'LL DO WHATEVER YOU TELL ME TO DO.

DIE!
철컥

쏴아아..

DAMN IT! WHY DID IT HAVE TO RAIN ON THE OPENING DAY OF MY CAFÉ?!
IT RAINS HERE DAY AND NIGHT.
PAMELA?
I WASN'T SURE, BUT IT IS YOU AFTER ALL.

WHAT HAPPENED? I CALLED YOU AGAIN AND AGAIN, BUT YOU NEVER ANSWERED. I THOUGHT SOMETHING TERRIBLE HAD HAPPENED TO YOU.

I THINK I HAD A BAD COLD OR SOMETHING. I SLEPT FOR THREE WHOLE DAYS.

WERE YOU WORRIED?

ARE YOU ALL RIGHT NOW?

WELL, NO...I JUST THOUGHT... SINCE YOU SAID YOU WERE SICK.

I KNEW THERE WAS SOMETHING SPECIAL ABOUT YOU THE MOMENT I SAW YOU.

YOU ARE LIKE A LITTLE GIRL AT TIMES...AND AT OTHER TIMES, A GROWN WOMAN...

I FEEL WE'RE BONDED IN SOME MYSTERIOUS WAY THAT I CAN'T FULLY UNDERSTAND...

I'M SORRY. I'LL STOP BY NEXT TIME. I HAVE TO GO NOW.

TA

1987 JULY
1993 FEBRUARY
HMM...DO YOU HAVE A SOFTER SIDE I DON'T KNOW ABOUT?
WERE YOU TAKING A STROLL DOWN MEMORY LANE?
WELCOME.
I WAS TOO YOUNG TO REMEMBER ANYTHING BEFORE I CAME TO LIVE WITH YOU.
WAS I FIVE YEARS OLD WHEN WE FIRST MET?

FOUR. YOU WERE WEARING A WHITE SHIRT WITH BLUE STRIPES.

I'M VERY GRATEFUL TO YOU... FOR RAISING ME LIKE YOUR OWN SON.

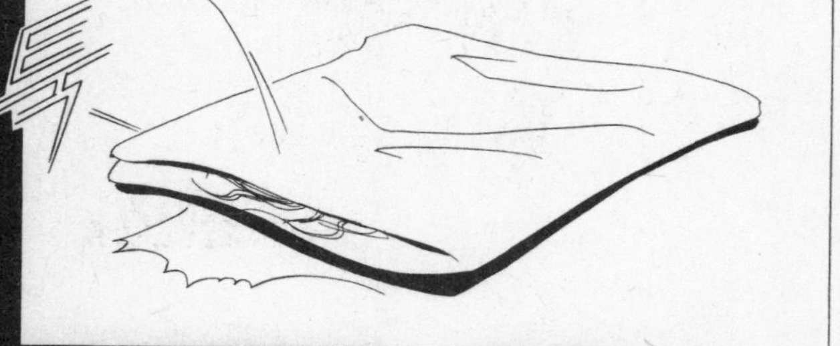
THIS IS A CLIPPING OF PAMELA'S HAIR.

I CAN LOOK INTO HER PAST WITH IT.
IT WILL SHOW ME THINGS THAT TAROT CARDS CANNOT.
WHAT IS IT THAT YOU WANT TO KNOW?

I CAN'T SHOW YOU EVERYTHING.

THERE'S A LIMIT TO HOW MUCH I CAN SEE.

I WANT TO KNOW HOW PAMELA AND BELUS MET.

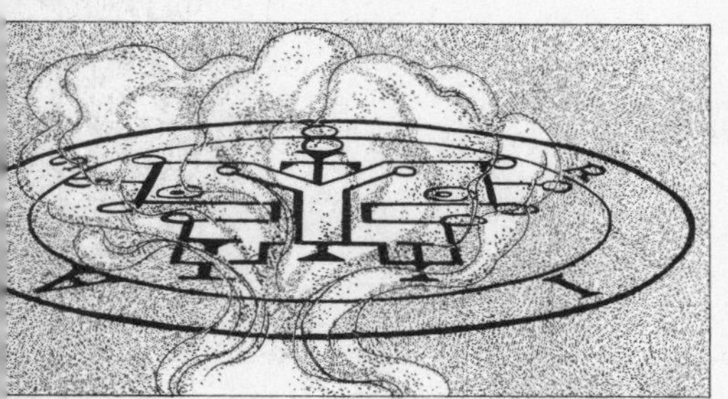

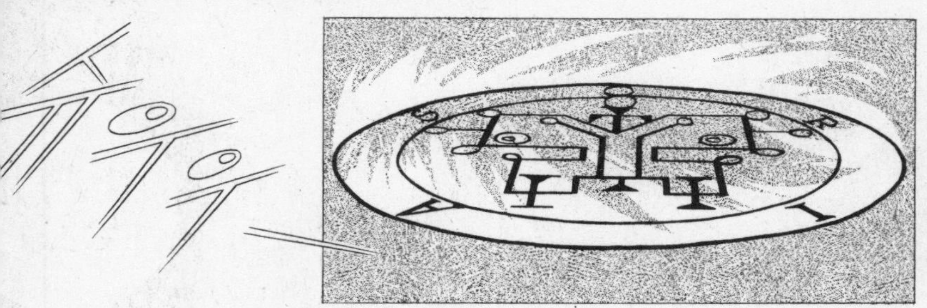

EACH TIME I FLIP OVER A CARD, A PIECE OF PAMELA'S PAST WILL BE REVEALED.

THROUGH A KIND OF ILLUSION..

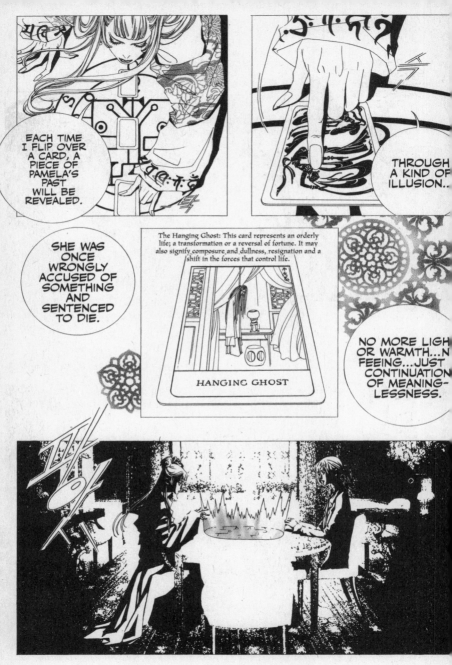

The Hanging Ghost: This card represents an orderly life; a transformation or a reversal of fortune. It may also signify composure and dullness, resignation and a shift in the forces that control life.

SHE WAS ONCE WRONGLY ACCUSED OF SOMETHING AND SENTENCED TO DIE.
HANGING GHOST
NO MORE LIGH OR WARMTH...N FEEING...JUST CONTINUATION OF MEANING-LESSNESS.

THAT SERVANT OF SATAN, THE DRAGON, IS DEAD.
NOW THE WITCH THAT COMMANDED THE DRAGON MUST FACE JUDGMENT.
DO YOU BELIEVE IN MAGIC?
I COULDN'T SAY ANYTHING.
SATAN HAS CAST A SPELL OVER YOU SO THAT YOU CANNOT SPEAK. YOUR TONGUE IS FROZEN.
WE'LL FIND OUT IF YOU'RE A WITCH OR NOT BY DOING A WATER BURIAL.

EVEN DEATH IS MEANINGLESS.

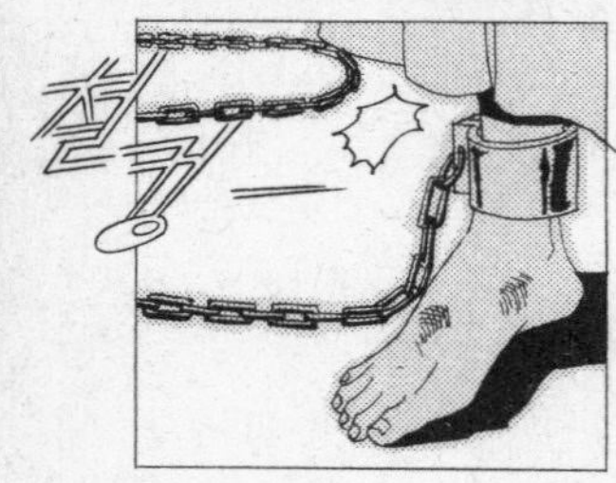
철컹

IF THIS WOMAN IS NOT A WITCH, SHE'LL SINK; IF SHE IS, THEN SHE'LL FLOAT ABOVE THE WATER WITH THE HELP OF SATAN.
ALONG WITH HIM, EVERYTHING SANK INTO AN ABYSS OF NOTHINGNESS...

YES...I'LL JOIN HIM IN DEATH...
I'M COMING, ASH.

POOR WAIF, SHE HAD NO ONE TO LEAN ON...
EIGHT OF CUPS
Eight of Cups: This card signifies letting go; finishing up and walking away. It may also mean that one is growing weary or seeking deeper meaning.

EVEN DEATH DID NOT WELCOME HER. SHE HAD TO EMBARK ON A LONG, LONELY JOURNEY BY HERSELF.

WHAT HAPPENED? I WAS JUST THROWN INTO THE SEA WITH A ROCK TIED AROUND MY ANKLE.

THOSE WHO COME IN CONTACT WITH THE FIRST DROP OF BLOOD FROM A DRAGON'S HEART...
...GAIN ETERNAL LIFE. THAT MARK ON YOUR FOREHEAD IS THE SIGN.

WHO ARE YOU?
YOU CAN'T DIE, EVEN IF YOU WANTED TO.

I'M THE PRINCE
OF PANDEMONIUM.
I'M BELUS.
I'VE COME
HERE TO
HELP YOU.

XI

ILLUSTRATION FROM MASTER TAROT

Vergebung
Forgiving

Forgiving: The ability to overcome one's sins by forgiving others.

WHY DID BELUS APPROACH PAMELA?

I DON'T KNOW...

THE BEGINNING OF A MEETING THAT HOLDS THE KEY TO ALL SECRETS...

Ace of Cups: This card represents letting your heart lead the way; trusting your inner voice; developing a relationship; letting your "love light" shine.

IT WAS THE BEGINNING OF A CONTRACT.

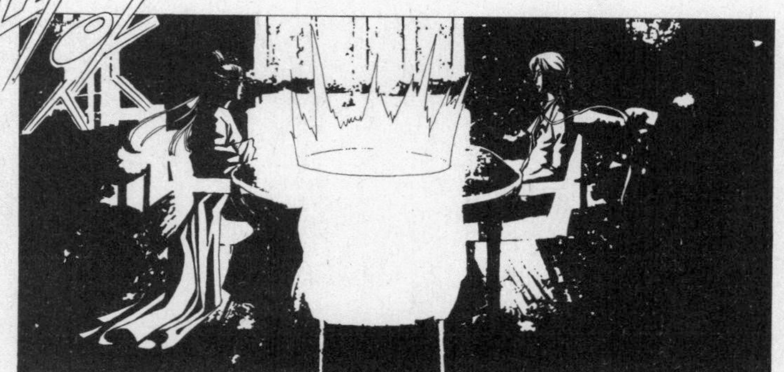

I DON'T KNOW WHETHER YOU'RE A MAN OR A MONSTER, BUT WHAT DID YOU MEAN BY WHAT YOU JUST SAID?
A MONSTER... YOU DARE CALL A BEAUTIFUL, YOUNG MAN LIKE ME A MONSTER?
I'M NOT IN THE MOOD FOR CHITCHAT.
JUST TELL ME WHAT YOU MEAN BY "THE BLOOD FROM A DRAGON'S HEART."
YOU'RE A FEISTY YOUNG LADY. IF YOU CHOOSE TO BEHAVE LIKE THAT, I MIGHT NOT TELL YOU ANYTHING.

TELL ME!
RIGHT NOW!
THERE SHE IS! THE WITCH CAME UP!
I CAN TAKE CARE OF MYSELF.
THEY'RE GOING TO BURN YOU AT THE STAKE OR CHOP OFF LIMBS, AND YOU WON'T EVEN DIE!
WHATEVER YOU SAY.

GOOD LUCK!
OKAY, I TAKE IT BACK! FORGET WHAT I SAID! HELP ME IF YOU'RE STILL THERE!
IF YOU APOLOGIZE FOR CALLING ME A MONSTER, I'LL THINK ABOUT IT.
I DON'T WANT TO BE BURNED TO DEATH!

MMMM...THE FLOWERS ARE SO FRAGRANT THIS TIME OF THE YEAR.

OKAY, OKAY, I MIGHT HAVE MADE A MISTAKE WHEN I CALLED YOU A MONSTER.

쩝쩝

AAAAH!

YES, OKAY! YOU'RE A BEAUTIFUL, YOUNG MAN!

YOU'RE THE MOST BEAUTIFUL MAN IN THE WORLD!

HEH HEH HEH.
AAAAAH!

AAAAAH!

WHAT ARE YOU DOING? PUT ME DOWN!
YOU ACT TOUGH, BUT YOU'RE JUST A GIRL, AFTER ALL. DON'T WORRY, YOU'RE NOT MY TYPE.
IDIOT! THAT'S NOT WHAT I MEANT! LOOK UNDERNEATH ME, FOR GOD'S SAKE!
MY ANKLE IS ABOUT TO SNAP!
묵직
OH, I'M SORRY.

뚝
쿵
OOPS, I'M SORRY.

THE DEVIL! THE DEVIL HAS COME!
LORD, HAVE MERCY ON YOUR FLOCK!
OH GOD, THE HANDS OF THE DEVIL HAVE REACHED US!

IT'S TOO NOISY HERE TO HAVE ANY SORT OF CONVERSATION.
LET'S GO SOMEWHERE QUIET.

BELUS' PREOCCUPATION WITH HIS LOOKS GOES BACK A LONG WAY.

AS DOES HIS PENCHANT FOR DRAMATIC APPEARANCE AND WRY HUMOR.
휘리리릭—

BY THE WAY, YOU SAID THAT A DRAGON WAS KILLED...BUT I THOUGHT NO HUMAN COULD DO THAT.

DECEPTIONS AND SECRETS ARE A WAY OF COMMUNICATION FOR THOSE WHO PLAY GAMES.

Ten of Staves: Right-side up, this card represents sure success, triumphant consolidation and danger of an established power becoming oppressive. Upside down, it signifies difficulty, conspiracy, betrayal and loss.

SOMEBODY IS UP TO SOMETHING NO GOOD...

WHAT HAPPENED?

YOU! DID YOU JUST USE ME?

IT'S YOUR OWN FAULT THAT YOU COULDN'T ACQUIRE THE DRAGON HEART OR THE WOMAN.

I GAVE YOU THE POWER TO SLAY DRAGONS.
AND YOU WERE ABLE TO KILL A RED DRAGON JUST AS YOU HAD WISHED.

Or should I say, kill her?
You were going to kill her if you couldn't have her, weren't you?

SHUT UP! NO MATTER--SINCE I DIDN'T GET MY WISH, OUR AGREEMENT IS OFF!

Ha ha ha.

You think you can tell me what to do?
When you signed over your soul to me, you didn't think about what you were really getting into, did you?
Stupid man...

HA...I'VE ALREADY DEDICATED MYSELF TO GOD. I JUST USED YOU FOR A BIT.
AND THE CONTRACT CLEARLY STATES, "WHEN ALL MY WISHES COME TRUE..."
I...I DON'T BELIEVE IT!
CONTRACT
I think you're mistaken, priest. There's no clause like that in the contract you signed.
Look very carefully.
Don't worry.
God has no need for a piece of trash like you, anyway.

I'LL SEE YOU IN HELL.

우적
우적

HELP YOURSELF TO MORE, IF YOU WANT.

CHANGE INTO THIS AFTER YOU'RE DONE EATING.

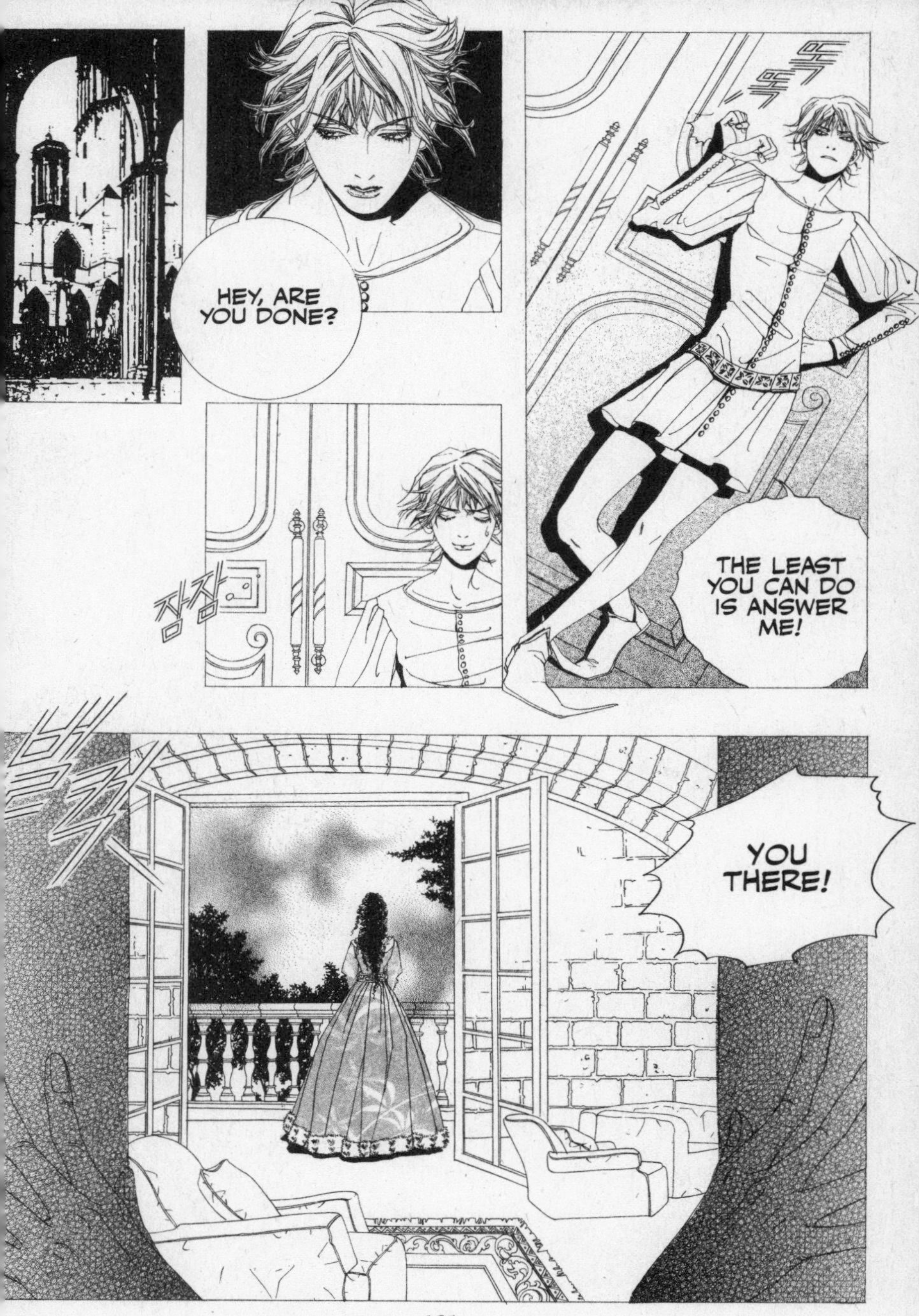
HEY, ARE YOU DONE?
똑 똑
THE LEAST YOU CAN DO IS ANSWER ME!
잠잠
벌컥
YOU THERE!

?
I'VE BEEN WITH ASH EVER SINCE.
WHEN I WAS ELEVEN, MY MOTHER WAS ACCUSED OF BEING A WITCH AND WAS BURNED AT THE STAKE.
HE RAISED ME...
...AND WAS MY TEACHER.
HE GAVE ME LOVE.
BUT HE DIED A HORRIBLE DEATH.

I HAD JUST EATEN A GOOD MEAL.
I SLEPT WELL, THEN GOT UP AND WASHED MYSELF.
DRESSED MYSELF, TALKED...
AND NOW I'M THINKING ABOUT WHAT WILL HAPPEN TO ME.
HE DIED...
AND NOW I CAN NO LONGER FEEL HIM.

YOU'RE ALIVE NOW.
AND YOU MUST GO ON LIVING.

WITHOUT *HIM*? LIVE WITHOUT *HIM*?!

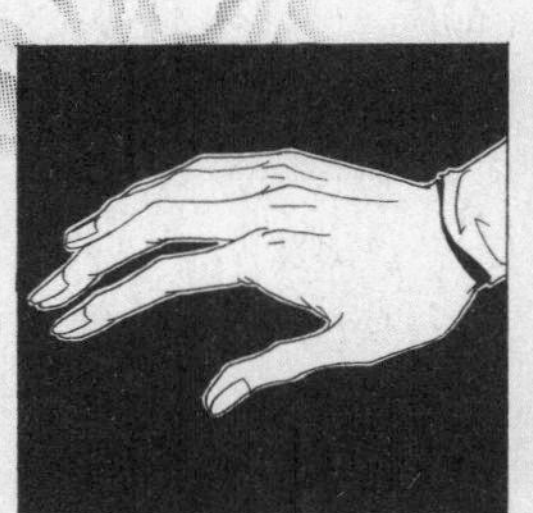

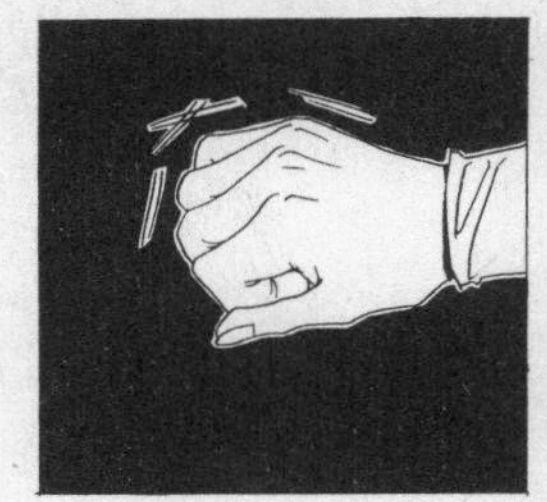

Die Verehrerin
The Devotee

The Devotee: Joyfully and willingly entrusting someone else with the task of making your wishes come true.

THE MOST IMPORTANT PART STILL REMAINS.
THE CONTRACT IS THE BEGINNING OF A JOURNEY.
Knight of Staves: Right-side up, this card signifies travel or progressing toward unknown territory. Upside down, it means unexpected change, skirmish, separation or dismissal.
KNIGHT OF STAVES
SHE WHO HAD LOWERED HER ANCHOR INTO THE SEA OF HER PAST MEMORIES...
...SHE CUT HERSELF LOOSE AND BEGAN A JOURNEY TOWARD A MYSTERIOUS FUTURE...

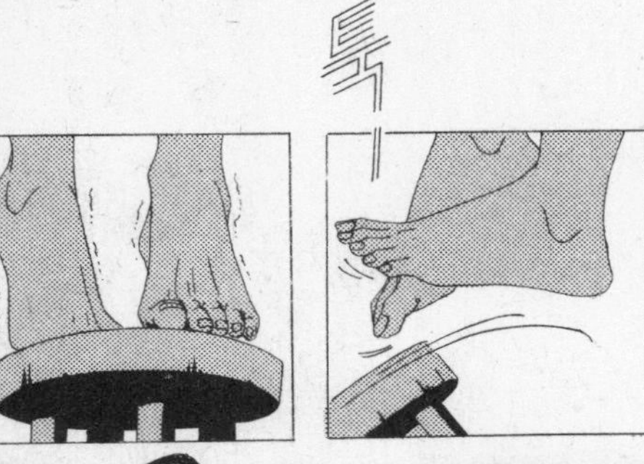
툭

CHOKE!
ACH!
GUH!

우르르쾅
번쩍

번쩍

LOOK, DON'T YOU THINK YOU'VE TRIED ENOUGH? YOU SHOULD KNOW BY NOW THAT NOTHING WORKS.

DON'T TRY TO STOP ME! LIFE WITHOUT ASH MEANS NOTHING TO ME.

I WASN'T TRYING TO STOP YOU. GO AHEAD, DO IT.

AAAAH!

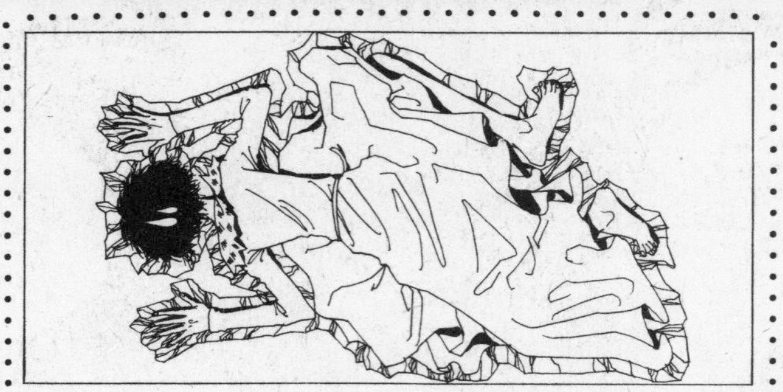

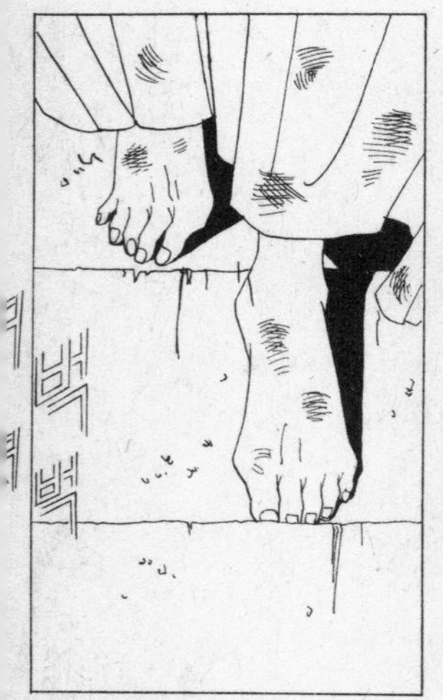

백
백

끼이이

NOW DO YOU FEEL LIKE TALKING?

끄덕 –
끄덕 –

DRAGONS ARE DIVINE, IMMORTAL BEINGS, LIKE GOD.
THE SOURCE OF THEIR POWER IS THEIR HEART.
THOUGH THEY CAN LIVE ETERNALLY, THEY CAN ALSO DIE IF CURSED BY A STRONGER BEING.
BLOOD OOZES FROM THEIR HEART AT THE TIME OF THEIR DEATH, AND THE PERSON WHO TOUCHES THAT FIRST DROP OF BLOOD...

...WILL NEVER GET OLD, SICK OR DIE.
IN OTHER WORDS, HE OR SHE WILL HAVE THE DRAGON'S IMMORTALITY.
SO I CAN'T DIE, NO MATTER HOW HARD I TRY.
AND THAT UPSETS YOU?
I FEEL NOTHING BUT EMPTINESS SINCE ASH DIED.
EVEN BREATHING IS HARD. NOTHING IS MEANINGFUL. I SEE NOTHING WORTH LIVING FOR.
YOU KNOW, THERE ARE PEOPLE WHO HUNT DRAGONS FOR THEIR POWER OF IMMORTALITY.
DO YOU REALLY WANT TO DIE?

SO YOU DO KNOW HOW I CAN DIE? I KNEW NOT EVERYONE HAS THE POWER TO FLY AND BREAK CHAINS WITH THEIR BARE HANDS, BUT...
ARE YOU SATAN?

WHAT DIFFERENCE DOES IT MAKE?

I GUESS NOT. WELL, I DON'T CARE IF YOU'RE THE DEVIL OR AN ANGEL, AS LONG AS YOU GRANT ME DEATH.

LET'S DRAW UP A CONTRACT, THEN.

DO YOU WANT MY SOUL OR SOMETHING?

HA HA... THE SOUL OF AN IMMORTAL HUMAN BEING?
I CAN GET A HUMAN SOUL WHENEVER I WANT.
NO, THERE'S SOMETHING I WANT MORE THAN THAT.
SOMETHING YOU WANT?
BERIAL'S NECKLACE.
THE NECKLACE BROKE, AND THE BEADS SCATTERED ALL OVER THE EARTH.
COLLECT THOSE BEADS FOR ME, AND IN RETURN, I WILL GIVE YOU DEATH. DO WE HAVE A DEAL?

THE CONTRACT?

HA HA HA.

WHAT?

I REALLY LIKE YOU.
CONTRACT

HMMM...SO THE TWO OF THEM ARE MERELY CONTRACTUAL PARTNERS?
PERHAPS IT'S NOT SO BLACK AND WHITE.
WHAT DO YOU THINK, THEN?
WELL...

SHOW ME HOW PAMELA FEELS ABOUT BELUS.
SHE DID SOMETHING NO ONE ELSE WAS ABLE TO DO. THAT WAS THE REASON BELUS NOTICED HER.
The Tower: This card represents unexpected disaster or an abrupt change in lifestyle that can lead to new realizations; change of opinion.
XVI
THE TOWER
INTEREST, GAZE, GOODWILL-- IT IS CERTAIN THAT BELUS LIKES PAMELA.
The Universe: This card represents perfection, completion, positive change, and achievement.
XVI
THE
I DON'T KNOW IF THAT AFFECTION IS PLATONIC OR ROMANTIC.

I GUESS SOMEONE DOESN'T LIKE US LOOKING INTO THE FUTURE.

?

BUT, CORA...

HMM... THAT'S ENOUGH.

THAT RAINY DAY...I STILL CAN'T REMEMBER WHAT HAPPENED. CAN YOU TELL ME?
I ALREADY TOLD YOU, I DON'T KNOW EXACTLY WHAT HAPPENED.
IS THAT SO?

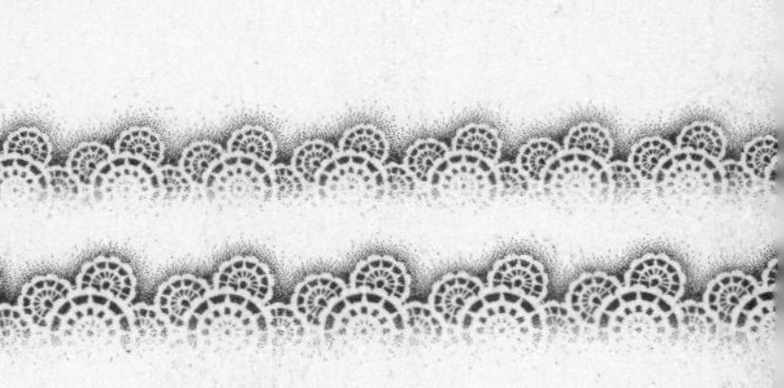

IF YOU LIE OR BETRAY ME, I WILL KILL YOU.

I'LL TRY TO REMEMBER THAT.

CHU

TAROT

YOU REALLY WANT TO KNOW?

WHAT?

NOTHING. LET'S PARTY!

EVERYONE WATCH OUT FOR THE CORK!
HEH HEH HEH HEH.

YES, PAMELA...
YOU ARE A STRONG AND BEAUTIFUL PERSON.

NO MATTER WHAT HAPPENS,

I HOPE YOU NEVER CHANGE.

OH, NO!
I CAN'T BELIEVE WE BROKE THE WINDOW THE FIRST DAY THE CAFÉ OPENED!

I WONDER WHO...

CENTR
Spring
fore

THAT'S STRANGE. THERE'S NO ONE OUTSIDE.

1 St
CENTRAAL
Spring 199
foresight
CAFE
TAROT
CENTRAAL
WHAT'S THIS?

탁

뚜벅
뚜벅

Episode 13: Leanan Sidhe (One)

Nine of pentacles

Nine of Pentacles: Right-side up, this card signifies self-discipline, self-reliance and enjoying the finer things in life. Upside down, it represents the loss of safety, theft and breakup.

ILLUSTRATION FROM TAROT OF OLD PATH

YOU NEED SOME HELP?
A WOMAN NAMED PAMELA CAN TELL YOU WHAT YOU WANT TO KNOW.
?

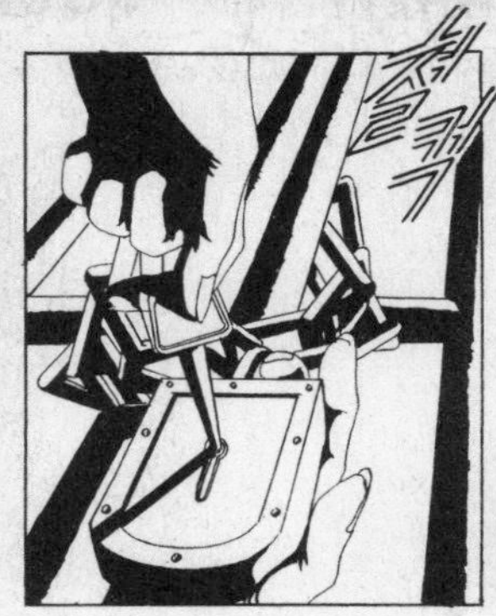

ON THE FIFTEENTH OF EACH MONTH, I LOSE CONTROL OF MYSELF AND I REMEMBER NOTHING.

IT'S BEEN LIKE THIS FOR A FULL YEAR.

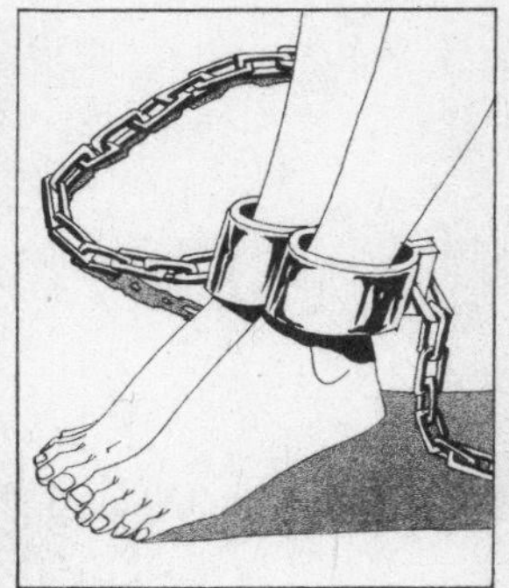

WHEN WILL I BE FREE OF THIS CURSE?
WHEN WILL I MEET NEBIROS AGAIN?

HOW IS HE?

SHOULD I GO CHECK?
STOP WORRYING AND JUST GET SOME SLEEP. IT'S NOTHING NEW.

BANG

GRRRRRR...
GRRRRRR...
HELLO, LITTLE KITTY. AREN'T YOU SICK AND TIRED OF BEING LOCKED UP?
GO OUT AND PLAY AS LONG AS YOU WANT!

I THINK I SHOULD GO DOWN AND CHECK ON HIM.
WHATEVER YOU WANT.

AARON?

OH, SHIT!

DO YOU HAVE ANY IDEA WHERE HE MIGHT HAVE GONE?

WE HAVE TO FIND HIM BEFORE SOMETHING TERRIBLE HAPPENS!

WAIT A MINUTE.

Ace of Cups: This card represents letting your heart lead the way and trusting your inner voice. It may also signify developing a relationship or letting your "love light" shine.

ACE OF CUPS

IS THERE A BIG CONCERT TODAY IN LONDON?

YES, SASHA'S CONCERT.

HE'S NUMBER ONE ON THE CHARTS. ALL THE CRITICS GAVE HIM FIVE STARS.

HE SELLS OUT 100,000 SEATS AT HIS CONCERTS.

ROAR!

WHAT IS THAT?
FOR A PROP, IT LOOKS SO REAL!

ROAR!
GRRRR!
할짝

WE'RE NOT TOO LATE.

NOPE, I THINK WE ARE A LITTLE TOO LATE.

GRRRR!
SOMEBODY HELP ME!
HOLD STILL, AARON.
YOU'RE ABOUT TO GET A VERY PAINFUL SHOT.
LUCKILY, THE CROWD THINKS THIS IS PART OF THE SHOW.

OH, SHIT...
HOW MANY BULLETS DID YOU BRING?
THE THREE I JUST USED.
ROAR!!!
!!!

퍽
퍽
퍽
와아
와아
와아

SO THAT LITTLE PUPPY BELONGS TO YOU?

하하

WHAT WERE YOU THINKING?! WHAT IF SOMETHING TERRIBLE HAD HAPPENED?

I'LL MAKE UP FOR IT. IF YOU'LL JUST KEEP QUIET ABOUT IT...

IN THAT CASE...

HAVE YOU EVER HEARD OF THE LEGEND OF LYANNONSHI?

I SEE.

ALL RIGHT.
THIS WILL PROBABLY BE USEFUL TO ME AS WELL.

I'M LUCKY TO HAVE MET SOMEONE LIKE YOU.

NO! NO! SEND THAT WOLF TO THE ZOO! WHY ARE YOU DOING THIS?

WHEN WILL I GET A CHANCE TO DO SOMETHING LIKE THIS AGAIN? TRY TO THINK POSITIVELY.

EVERYTHING WORKED OUT AFTER ALL.

I FEEL BAD FOR BELUS, BUT...

ARE YOU PAMELA?

YOU CAME ALL THE WAY HERE IN SEARCH OF YOUR DEBTOR.
Justice: This card represents a sense of balance in life; taking responsibility for one's actions; doing what is right.
JUSTICE
Yes.
BUT YOU...
Eight of Rods: This card signifies a push towards a desired outcome; finding the missing piece of the puzzle. It can also mean completing unfinished business or putting one's plans into action.
EIGHT OF RODS

THE NECKLACE AND BRACELETS I WEAR REPRESENT PAYMENT MADE FROM THE PEOPLE WHO DEALT WITH ME.

HAVE YOU HEARD OF A SPRITE THAT GIVES INSPIRATION TO ARTISTS AND THEN TAKES AWAY THEIR LIVES IN RETURN?

THE PERSON I'M LOOKING FOR IS A POPULAR SINGER NAMED SASHA. YOU'VE PROBABLY HEARD OF HIM.

WHAT A COINCIDENCE! THIS IS THE SAME STORY I HEARD AN HOUR AGO.

UNTIL A FEW MONTHS AGO, I WAS JUST AN UNKNOWN SINGER.

AREN'T YOU CURIOUS TO KNOW HOW I BECAME SO FAMOUS?

This is Not All...!

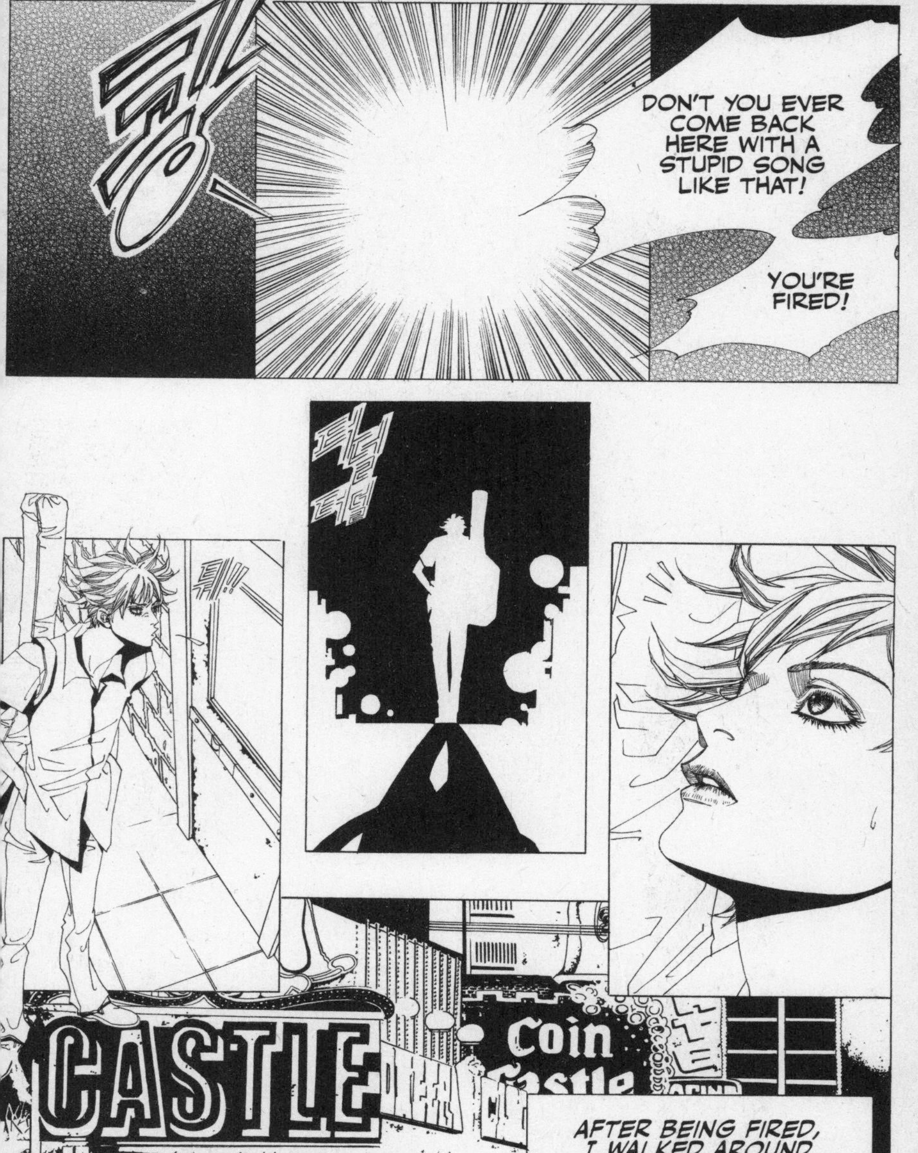

AFTER BEING FIRED, I WALKED AROUND AIMLESSLY, FEELING LIKE A REAL PIECE OF SHIT. THEN I WENT INTO A BAR FOR A DRINK...

KURT... KURT COBAIN?

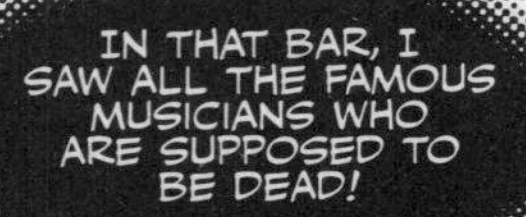
IN THAT BAR, I SAW ALL THE FAMOUS MUSICIANS WHO ARE SUPPOSED TO BE DEAD!

JOHN LENNON.

JIM MORRISON.

JOHN DENVER.

ELVIS PRESLEY.

......

Carlsberg
Beer Biere

WE BECAME BUDDY-BUDDY WHILE DISCUSSING MUSIC.

PERHAPS YOU'RE CURIOUS HOW I CAME TO BE SO SUCCESSFUL?

?

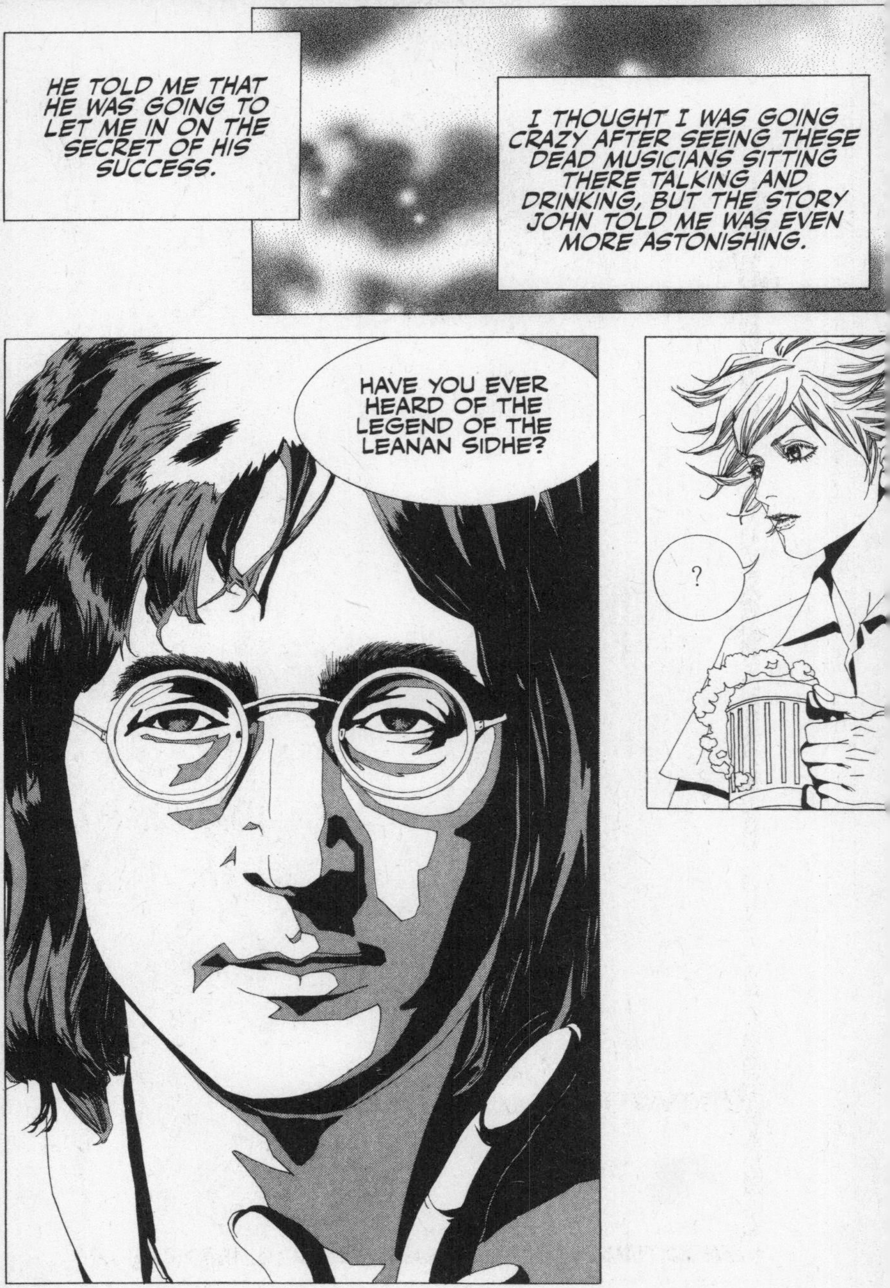

HE TOLD ME THAT HE WAS GOING TO LET ME IN ON THE SECRET OF HIS SUCCESS.

I THOUGHT I WAS GOING CRAZY AFTER SEEING THESE DEAD MUSICIANS SITTING THERE TALKING AND DRINKING, BUT THE STORY JOHN TOLD ME WAS EVEN MORE ASTONISHING.

HAVE YOU EVER HEARD OF THE LEGEND OF THE LEANAN SIDHE?

ILLUSTRATION FROM TAROT OF OLD PATH

Page of Cauldrons: Right-side up, this card represents someone with an artistic gift; someone prone to contemplation. Upside down, it represents a girl or a boy with light brown hair; a youth with extreme intelligence.

A LEANAN SIDHE IS A SPRITE THAT GIVES ARTISTIC INSPIRATION IN RETURN FOR YOUR LIFE.
SHE SEDUCES ARTISTS WITH HER BEAUTY.
AS YOU CAN SEE, THE PEOPLE GATHERED HERE WERE ALL SUCCESSFUL MUSICIANS IN LIFE, BUT ULTIMATELY HAD TO FAKE THEIR OWN DEATH.
HOW CAN I EXPLAIN IT? WE'RE DEAD AS SOON AS WE ARE FOUND ALIVE.

I THINK I DRANK QUITE A BIT WHILE TALKING TO HIM.
I DON'T EVEN REMEMBER HOW I GOT HOME.
AND THEN I FOUND HER.
DON'T YOU WANT TO BE A STAR?
WHEN I WENT BACK THE NEXT DAY, THE BAR HAD VANISHED.
I CAN'T EXPLAIN HOW I STUMBLED INTO THAT BAR, OR HOW I FOUND THE LEANAN SIDHE. I DON'T UNDERSTAND IT MYSELF.
PERHAPS MY DESIRE FOR SUCCESS MADE EVERYTHING POSSIBLE.

WHEN SHE WAS WITH ME, I FELT AS IF A MUSE WAS WHISPERING HEAVENLY TUNES INTO MY EAR.
I COMPOSED ONE SONG AFTER ANOTHER.

IN TIME, WE BECAME QUITE CLOSE.
BUT I NEVER FORGOT WHAT JOHN LENNON HAD TOLD ME.

SASHA'S RECORD GOES GOLD!
SASHA IS NAMED THE MUSICIAN OF THE 21ST CENTURY!
Hot & Single
ROCK& ROLL
SASHA HAS THE NUMBER-ONE RECORD 15 WEEKS IN A ROW!

AS EACH ONE OF MY WISHES CAME TRUE...
BUT...
THE DAY I REACHED THE PINNACLE OF MY CAREER, I WAS SUPPOSED TO SURRENDER MY SOUL TO HER.
WHAT'S WRONG WITH YOU?
I BEGAN TO SUFFER FROM SEVERE ANXIETY ATTACKS.

HER NECKLACE AND BRACELETS-- THESE WERE PAYMENTS FROM THE MEN WHO ENTERED INTO BARGAINS WITH HER.
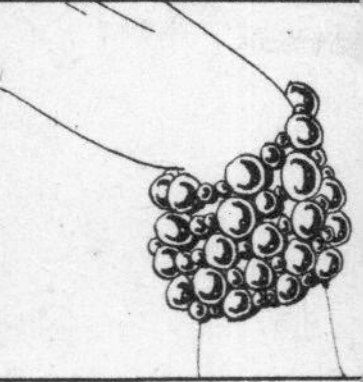

SHE WAS GOING TO TURN ME INTO A SINGLE BEAD ON HER NECKLACE WHEN I REACHED MY GOAL.

HER ONE WEAKNESS IS THE NECKLACE AND THE BRACELETS SHE WEARS. THE BEADS ON THEM REPRESENT THE SOULS OF THE MEN WHO BARTERED THEIR LIVES FOR HER ARTISTIC INSPIRATION.
THEY ARE LIKE HER HEART. IF YOU BREAK THEM, SHE WILL BE IMMOBILIZED FOR A SHORT TIME. GOOD LUCK TO YOU.
......

뒤척
MMMM...

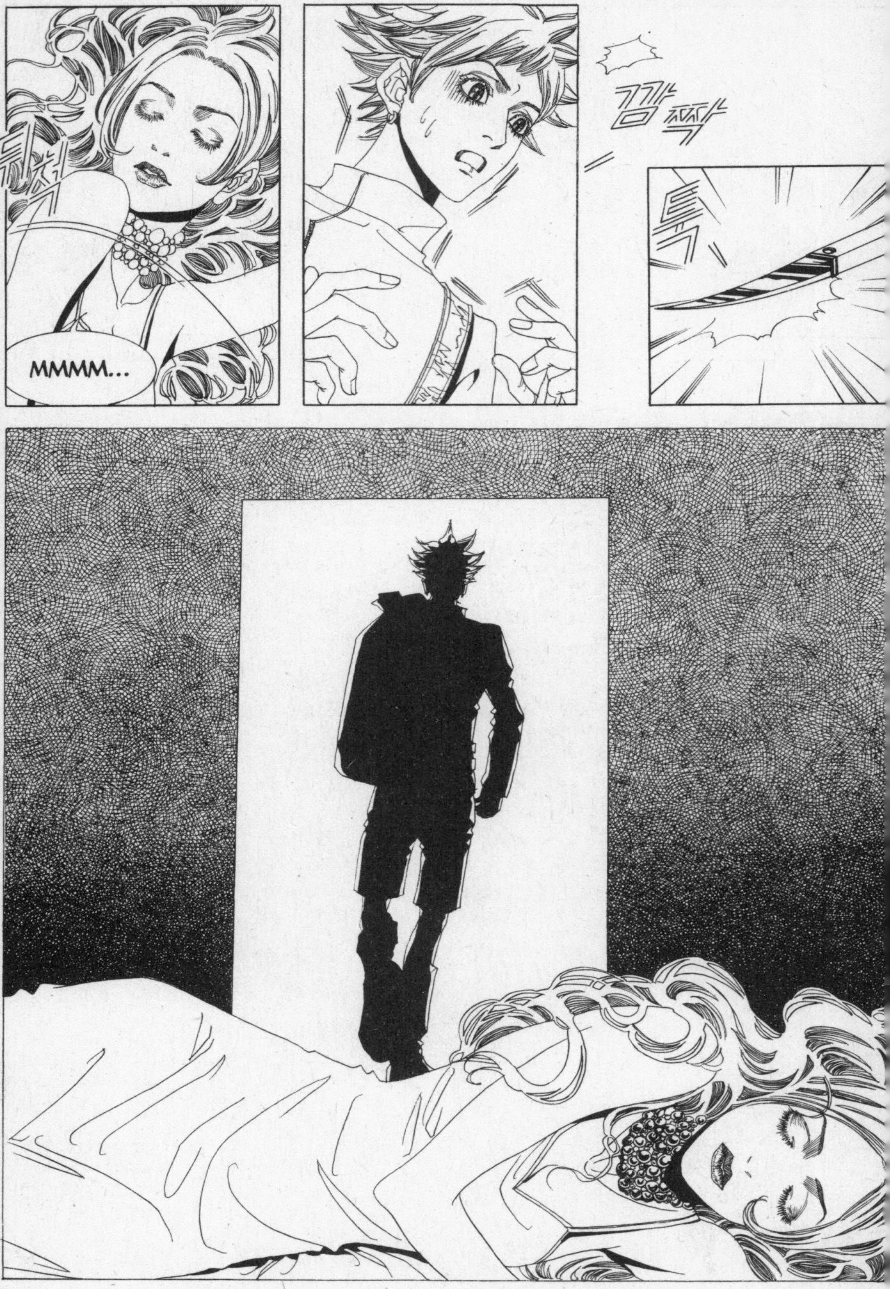

깜짝

툭

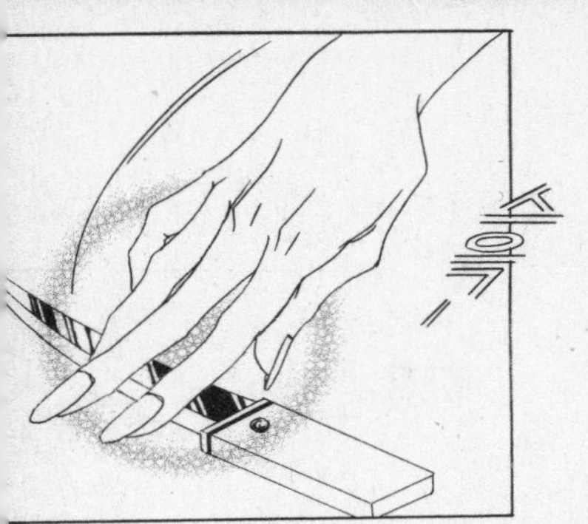

YOU KNOW VERY WELL THAT YOU CAN'T CANCEL THE LONDON CONCERT! I DON'T EVEN NEED TO REMIND YOU THE GRAMMY AWARDS ARE COMING UP.

REMEMBER WHAT YOU'VE WORKED SO HARD FOR!

THE BEATLES, THE ROLLING STONES, RADIOHEAD, ETC, ETC....

THE GRAMMYS ESTABLISHED THEM AS TOP MUSICIANS... AND THAT'S WHY I WORKED SO HARD...

ALL RIGHT, I'LL DO THE CONCERT AND GO TO THE GRAMMYS. BUT I'M GOING TO LEAVE TEN MINUTES BEFORE THE END OF THE CEREMONY. YOU FILL IN THE GAP AS BEST YOU CAN.

WHY ARE YOU ACTING LIKE THIS?! YOU OWE ME AN EXPLANATION AT LEAST.

I DON'T EVEN KNOW WHY I'M STILL ALIVE. I JUST RAN AWAY.
This is Not All
WHAT ARE YOU THINKING ABOUT?

YES, HE TURNED OUT TO BE A LITTLE DIFFERENT THAN I EXPECTED.

딱딱딱딱...
STOP RIGHT THERE!
거기서!!
딱딱딱
탁탁탁

?!!
AAAAAH!

트득 트득 트득
멈칫
HELP, HELP ME...

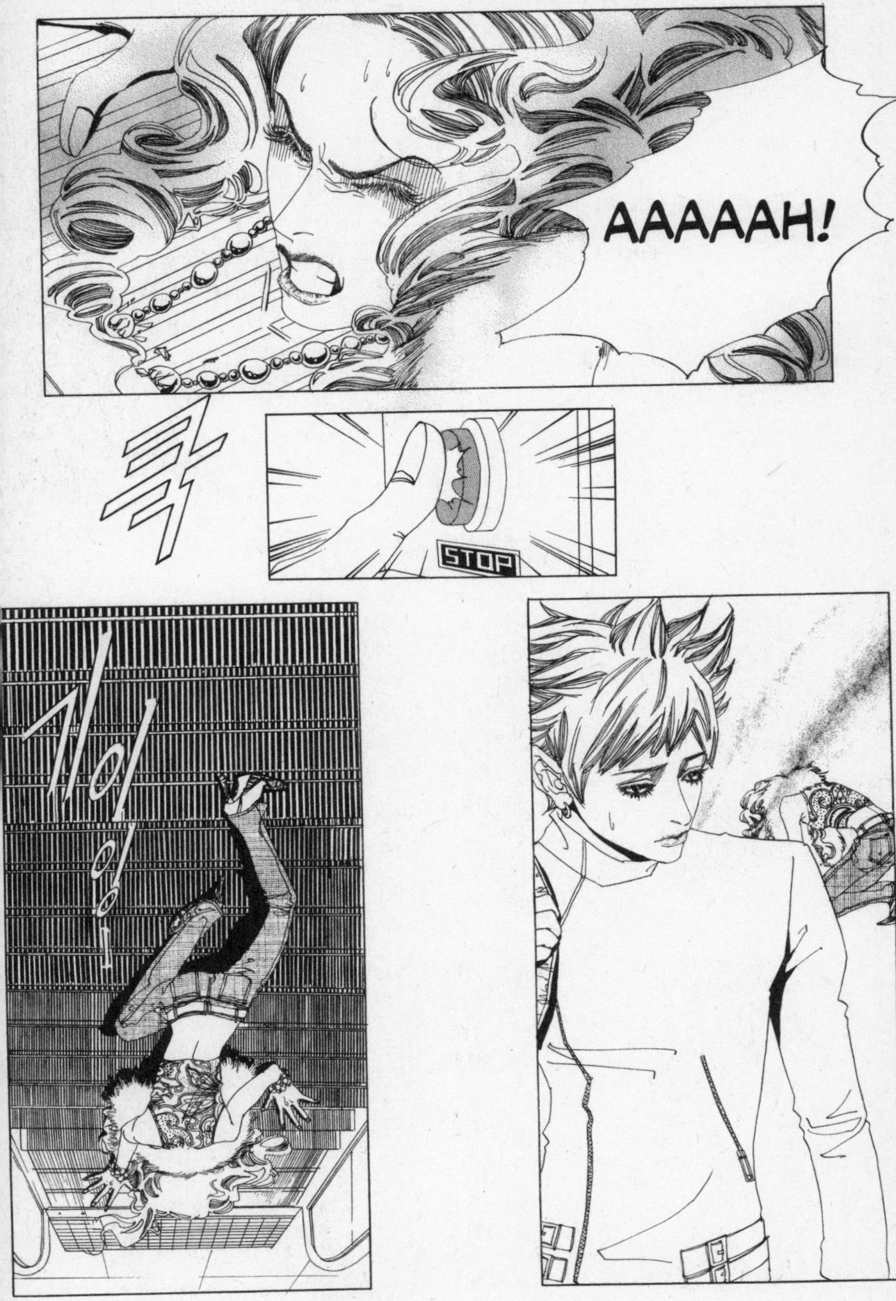

AAAAAH!

쿡

STOP

STANDING ON TOP...
XIX
The Sun: Right-side up, this card represents understanding, satisfaction, liberation and achieving one's goals. Upside down, it represents an uncertain future or the loss of something valuable.

TOMORROW HE WILL WIN A GRAMMY.
WHAT ARE YOU GOING TO DO? SASHA SAVED YOU, AFTER ALL.
WELL...

I'M CURIOUS ABOUT SOMETHING.

?

THANK YOU. I MUST GO NOW.

IT'S A SMALL WORLD.

LAST YEAR, THE GRAMMY AWARDS WAS BROADCAST IN 170 COUNTRIES. OVER 1.5 BILLION PEOPLE WATCHED THE BIGGEST CELEBRATION IN MUSIC.
NOW, IN ITS 46TH YEAR, THE GRAMMY AWARDS...

와아, 와아

ARE YOU FEELING ALL RIGHT? YOU DON'T LOOK SO GOOD.
I'M ALL RIGHT. I JUST HAVE A BIT OF A HEADACHE.

……

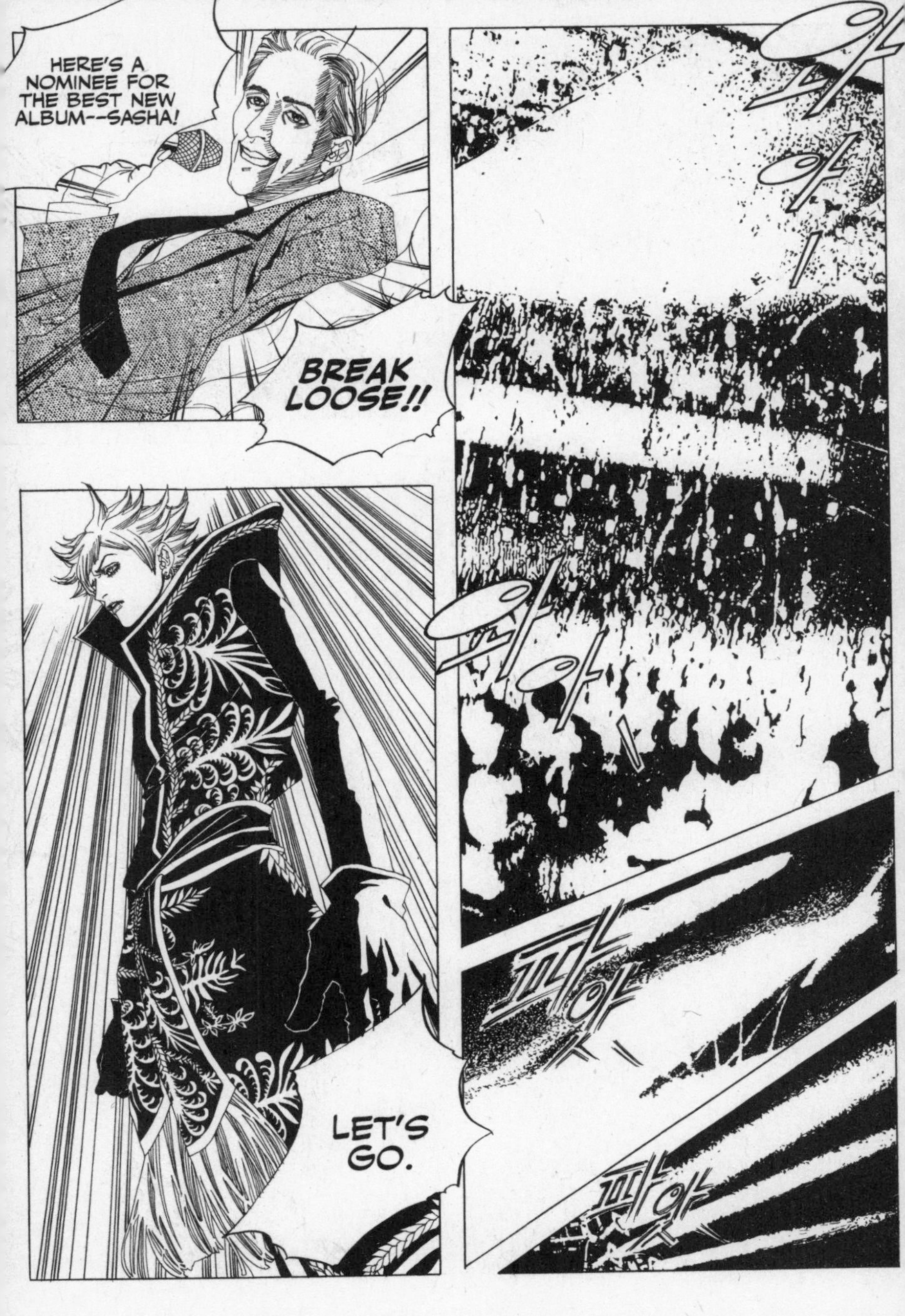
HERE'S A NOMINEE FOR THE BEST NEW ALBUM--SASHA!
BREAK LOOSE!!
LET'S GO.

Leanan Sidhe (Two)

ILLUSTRATION FROM TAROT OF OLD PATH.

*Ten of Swords: This card signifies the ruin and defeat that can follow a person; disappointment, pain, tears and jealousy.

THIS MOMENT IS LIKE THE FIRST SPARK FROM A LIT MATCH.
...I HAVE NO REGRETS OR WORRIES.

ARE YOU LISTENING, LEANAN? THIS ONE'S FOR YOU.
BECAUSE IT'S THE LAST SONG I'LL EVER SING.
OH, I'M LISTENING. WITH GRATITUDE...
NOTHING IS FREE IN THIS WORLD.
SCARY.

HE'S DISAPPEARED!

TIME TO PAY UP, SASHA.

PLEASE, WON'T YOU RECONSIDER?
투둑

LAST NIGHT AT THE 45TH GRAMMY AWARDS, THE SINGER SASHA FELL TO HIS DEATH DURING HIS FIRST PERFORMANCE.
SASHA HAD BEEN NOMINATED FOR NINE CATEGORIES, AND HAD HE LIVED, WOULD HAVE TAKEN HOME EIGHT OF THE AWARDS.
L.A. TIMES.
CESYA,
DEAD

SASHA, WHO MANY CONSIDERED TO BE THE BEST SINGER OF OUR TIME...
...DIED IN THE PRIME OF HIS LIFE.
I WONDER IF HIS DYING SO YOUNG IS A BREACH OF CONTRACT. HE NEVER ACTUALLY REACHED THE TOP OF HIS CAREER...
HA HA HA...

CAFE
TAROT
SOMETIMES EVEN YOU CAN COME IN HANDY, BELUS.

I KNOW I'M IMMORTAL, BUT FALLING LIKE THAT STILL HURTS LIKE A SON-OF-A-BITCH!
!!
LOOK AT THIS LUMP. IT'S THE SIZE OF MY FIST!
IT'S BETTER THAN BURNING TO DEATH, GETTING ELECTROCUTED, OR DROWNING, ISN'T IT?
WHEN WAS IT THAT YOU TOOK OVER FOR SASHA?
파삭
JUST AS HE DISAPPEARED INTO THE FLAMES, I APPEARED FROM ABOVE.
WASN'T IT *SO* COOL?
YEAH, BUT THROWING THAT FLOWER WAS WAY CHEESY.
I GUESS YOU CAN'T HELP BEING DRAMATIC, BUT AT LEAST TRY TO BE ORIGINAL NEXT TIME.
I THOUGHT IT WAS ROMANTIC. YOU... YOU LOOKED LIKE A PRINCESS LAST NIGHT.

SHOULD I BECOME A SINGER, TOO? I MISS IT, YOU KNOW. WHEN I SAW THE AUDIENCE CHEERING, I UNDERSTOOD HOW SASHA COULD HAVE RISKED HIS LIFE BY MAKING A DEAL WITH LEANAN.
You win!!
OH PLEASE, WILL YOU STOP LOOKING AT ME LIKE THAT? I THINK YOUR OLD FACE FITS BETTER WITH THAT IMAGINATION OF YOURS!

WHATEVER! AT FIRST, YOU WERE LIKE AN ANIMAL GETTING DRAGGED TO THE SLAUGHTER-HOUSE.

WHAT DO YOU EXPECT? IT'S BETTER THAN WEARING A RUBBER MASK, RIGHT?

YOU'RE A NATURAL AT DECEIVING PEOPLE--YOU DON'T NEED SOMETHING LIKE THIS.

DO YOU HAVE TO SAY THINGS LIKE THAT? FOR YOU, I STILL....
CAN'T YOU SEE THE BANDAGE AROUND MY HEAD?

HELLO?
SHE'S NOT LISTENING.

I WAS WONDERING WHY LEANAN ASKED ME THAT.
TEN OF RODS: This card represents being pressured to succeed, or achievement that turns into toilsome burden. It signifies that one needs to lighten their load.
TEN OF RODS

IN HINDSIGHT, I THINK I KNOW WHY SHE DID WHAT SHE DID.
TWO OF SWORDS: In a situation where trouble may arise, a time of peace will follow.
TWO OF SWORDS

SHE *LOVED* HIM. SHE KNEW HE'D DECEIVED HER AND RUN AWAY, BUT SHE CHOSE TO LET IT PASS.
THE QUESTION SHE ASKED THEN...

THERE IS ONE THING I'M STILL CURIOUS ABOUT.

WERE HIS FEELINGS FOR ME GENUINE?

OF COURSE. SASHA LOVED HER, TOO.

THE FOOL: Positive inner power that influences one's choices.
FOOL
THEY JUST DIDN'T KNOW HOW TO EXPRESS THEIR FEELINGS FOR ONE ANOTHER.
THAT'S WHY HE COULDN'T WALK AWAY FROM THE ESCALATOR ACCIDENT, EVEN THOUGH HE KNEW SHE WOULD EVENTUALLY HARM HIM.

GREAT. NOW, I'LL PROBABLY GO BACK TO BEING ALLEY SCUM AGAIN.
IT'S KIND OF LIKE PRESSING THE "RESET" BUTTON DURING A VIDEO GAME.

FROM NOW ON, I'M GOING TO PROVE I CAN MAKE GOOD THINGS HAPPEN BY MY OWN INNER STRENGTH.

WHETHER OR NOT I SUCCEED ISN'T IMPORTANT ANYMORE.

WHAT MATTERS IS THAT I CAN BE WHO I *TRULY* AM.

HER ONLY WEAKNESS IS THE NECKLACE AND BRACELET SHE WEARS. DESTROY THOSE AND YOU CAN BE FREE OF HER. BUT IF YOU FAIL, YOUR ONLY WAY OUT IS TO FAKE YOUR OWN DEATH. THAT'S WHAT WE HAD TO DO.

GOOD LUCK.

REGARDLESS OF WHETHER MY NAME IS SASHA OR RAY SPACEY.

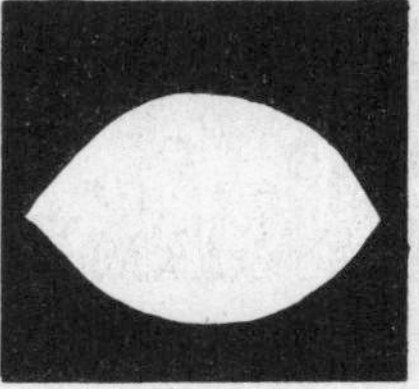

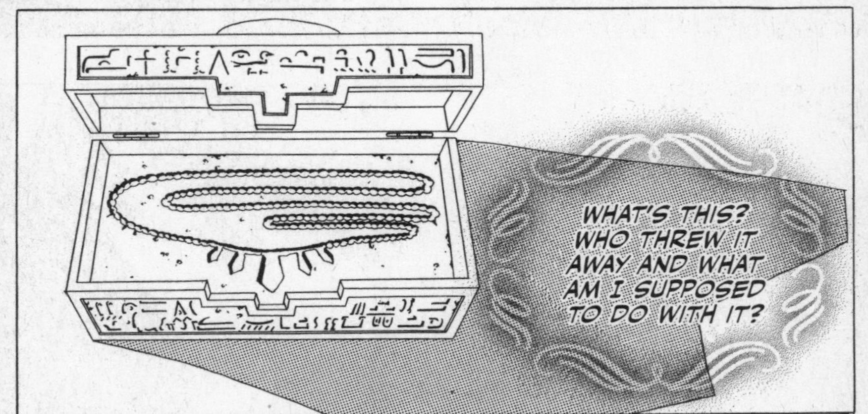
WHAT'S THIS? WHO THREW IT AWAY AND WHAT AM I SUPPOSED TO DO WITH IT?

PLACE ALL THE BEADS YOU'VE COLLECTED IN THE BOX.

WHO *ARE* YOU?

THEN YOU WILL BE ABLE TO SEE THE THINGS YOU COULDN'T BEFORE.

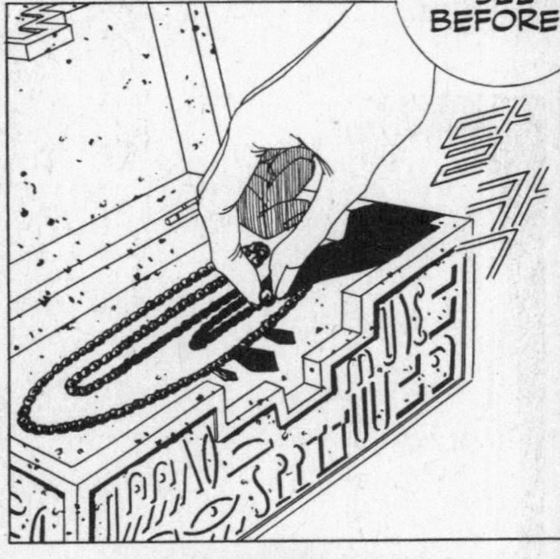

MEMORIES YOU HAVE FORGOTTEN...

I SEE YOU.
DIRTY, VILE... DISTORTED.
YOU'RE NO SAINT.

THAT'S ME
WHEN I WAS
YOUNG?

...WHO IS THAT PERSON?
...THOSE EYES...
THEY LOOK SO FAMILIAR.

THAT'S THE REASON YOU ARE IMMORTAL AND WHY YOU LOST THE ONES YOU LOVED.
EACH TIME YOU PUT ANOTHER BEAD IN THAT BOX, YOU'LL BE ABLE TO SEE ANOTHER TRUTH ABOUT WHO YOU ARE.
EVEN THE IDENTITY OF THE BEING THAT IS CONTROLLING YOUR LIFE.
WHAT DO YOU MEAN?

WAIT! WHAT DO YOU MEAN?!
THERE'S SOMEONE CONTROLLING MY LIFE?

탁

ILLUSTRATION FROM THE HERBAL TAROT DECK

*The Magician: This card represents the power of creation, achievement and infinite possibility.

PARFUM

IT'S TRUE. IF YOUR HUSBAND SPRAYS THIS SCENT, ANY WOMAN WHO SMELLS IT...

...WILL IMMEDIATELY DIE AT THE HANDS OF HER LOVER. INTERESTED? HEH HEH HEH...

WELCOME. CAN I HELP YOU?
I CAME HERE TO BUY SOME PERFUME, BUT I ALSO CAME TO SELL YOU SOMETHING YOU'VE BEEN LOOKING FOR.
?

HAVEN'T YOU BEEN HUNTING FOR AN IMMORTAL HUMAN?

THE KIND THAT BRINGS BACK FORGOTTEN MEMORIES!
I SEE. SO, THE PERFUME YOU WANT IS...?

CAFE
TAROT
Spring 1985

PAMELA, I HAD A STRANGE DREAM RECENTLY.

YEAH?

SOMEONE-- I CAN'T REMEMBER WHO- -WAS LOOKING DOWN ON ME WITH A FRIENDLY GAZE. THEY SO SEEMED FAMILIAR.

THERE WAS A TIME WHERE I HAD DREAMS LIKE THAT EVERY NIGHT.

LOOK, IT'S PERFUME YOU WEAR AROUND YOUR NECK. I THOUGHT IT WOULD LOOK NICE ON YOU.
HERE, LET ME PUT IT ON YOU.
THANK YOU. IT SMELLS GOOD!
IS IT CITRUS?
WHAT WERE YOU THINKING ABOUT SO INTENTLY?
OH... I WAS THINKING ABOUT GOING TO SCOTLAND.
SCOTLAND?

뚜벅 뚜벅
BE CAREFUL... YOU CAN'T RUN A SUCCESSFUL BUSINESS IF YOU TAKE OFF ALL THE TIME. THE CAFÉ WILL CLOSE DOWN!
WHY SCOTLAND?
LOOK: THE JESTER CARD SIGNIFIES THE BEGINNING OF A JOURNEY.
THE FOOL: this card can represent the beginning of an adventure; heading into the unknown.
EVEN IF THE TRIP COULD BE DANGEROUS, THE JESTER STILL HAS TO GO.
JOURNEYS ARE MIRRORS THAT REFLECT THE PAST.
THE TOWER: this card represents unexpected disaster or an abrupt change in lifestyle that can lead to new realizations or the possibility of repentance.
TOWER
IN SCOTLAND, I CAN GET THE ANSWERS TO SOME QUESTIONS AND FIND OUT THINGS THAT ARE GOING TO HAPPEN IN MY FUTURE.
THESE ANSWERS MIGHT SHAKE ME UP A BIT...
THE HERMIT: this card signifies the contemplation of the meaning of life; looking for answers within. It could also signify regret.
BUT THEY WILL ULTIMATELY SHOW ME THE WAY.

YOU KNOW, SOMEONE SHOWED ME SOMETHING ONCE...WHAT WAS IT? I NEED TO GO HOME TO FIND OUT...
WANT SOME COMPANY?
I'VE ALWAYS WANTED TO GO TO SCOTLAND!
LET ME GO WITH YOU!
THANKS, EVERYBODY, BUT I THINK IT'S BEST I GO BY MYSELF.
DON'T WORRY ABOUT THE CAFE I'LL TAKE GOOD CARE OF IT WHILE YOU'RE GONE.
THANKS, AARON.
HAVE THE TWO OF YOU MET?

......

THIS IS ASH.

I'M SURE WE'LL BE GOOD FRIENDS.

WELL THEN, HAVE A GOOD TRIP.

THIS SUCKS. WE HAVE TO GO TOGETHER NEXT TIME!
THANKS FOR SEEING ME OFF.

HAVE A GOOD TIME.

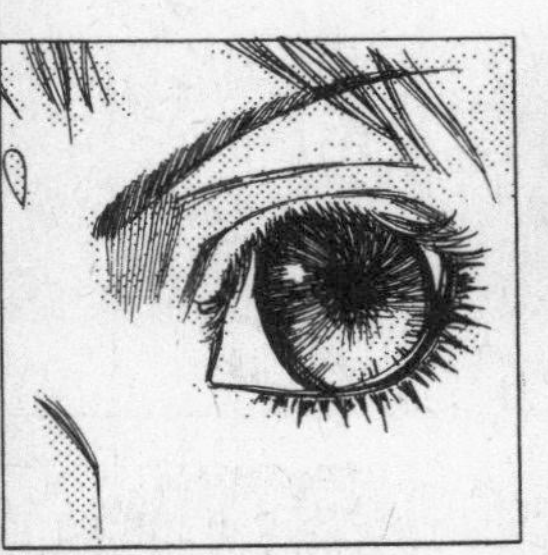

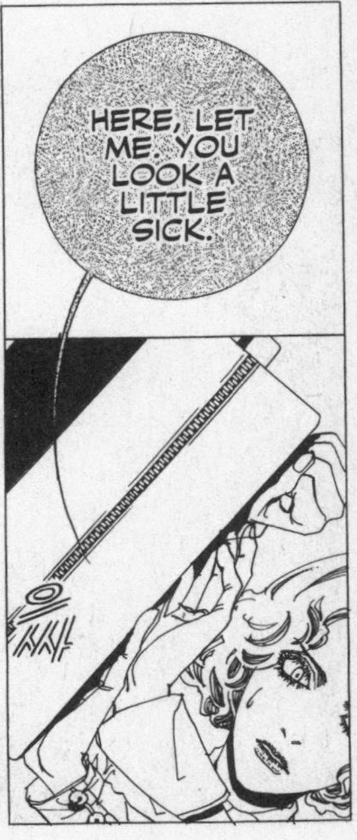
HERE, LET ME. YOU LOOK A LITTLE SICK.

OH, THANK YOU. YOU'RE RIGHT, I'M NOT FEELING TOO WELL.

HOW FAR ARE YOU GOING?

TO A SMALL VILLAGE OUTSIDE OF INVERNESS. YOU?

I'M HEADED THAT WAY, TOO. WHY ARE YOU GOING THERE?

TO SEE THE TRUTH.

AH, YOU READ TAROT CARDS? CAN YOU DO MY READING?

LET'S SEE...

THE EMPRESS

THE EMPRESS: This card signifies an abundance of body or mind; leadership, action, and good fortune.

HMM...THIS CARD SIGNIFIES ABUNDANCE, BUT IT CAN ALSO MEAN GREED.

IN THAT CASE, YOU SHOULD PURSUE MENTAL ABUNDANCE LIKE THE HIGH PRIESTESS.
HIGH PRIESTESS

HIGH PRIESTESS: This card represents the feminine principles of love and relationships. She is the ideal wife and mother that gives strength to those she loves; wonder, wisdom, and influence that doesn't show externally.

I DON'T UNDERSTAND WHAT THAT MEANS.
THIS HAS TO DO WITH YOUR INNER-SELF. THINK ABOUT IT FOR A WHILE AND IT WILL COME TO YOU.

HO HO...

THAT WAS FUN.
MAYBE IT WILL BE
OUR IN DESTINY TO
SEE EACH OTHER
AGAIN.

I TOLD MYSELF I'D NEVER COME BACK TO THIS PLACE...
A BAGEL AND A BLACK TEA, PLEASE.

뚜벅
WHAT'S THIS? YOU'RE ACTING LIKE A FATHER, HIDING HERE AND WATCHING OVER HER. IT MAKES ME WANT TO PUKE.
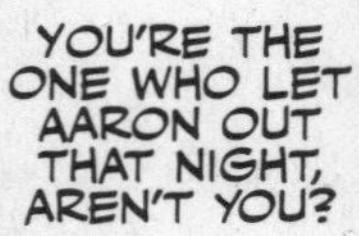

YOU'RE THE ONE WHO LET AARON OUT THAT NIGHT, AREN'T YOU?

IT WASN'T AS FUN AS I THOUGHT IT WOULD BE. ARE YOU HERE BECAUSE YOU THOUGHT I'D DO SOMETHING TO HARM PAMELA?

DID YOU DO SOMETHING TO HARM HER?

IT REALLY DOESN'T MATTER, EITHER WAY; SHE CAN'T DIE. ALTHOUGH SHE'D BE BETTER OFF IF SHE *WERE* DEAD.
HOO HOO...
I'M WARNING YOU: IF ANY HARM COMES TO PAMELA BY YOUR HAND, I'LL MAKE YOUR LIFE MISERABLE.
OOOH, I'M *SOOO* SCARED. YOU MUST REALLY LOVE HER, HUH?
POWER

THAT'S NONE OF YOUR CONCERN.

YOU OBVIOUSLY CARE ABOUT HER SAFETY, THOUGH.

!!

TLET
STOP!
THAT IS, IF I'M NOT IMAGINING THINGS...MAYBE SOMETHING'S WRONG WITH MY EYES.

AH, THANK YOU.

I KNEW THERE WAS NOTHING WRONG WITH MY EYESIGHT!

AND THIS PLACE!

뚜벅 뚜벅!

DON'T HIDE LIKE A COWARD! COME OUT WHERE I CAN SEE YOU!
UGH... WHY DO I FEEL DIZZY?
뚜벅 뚜벅

꿀꺽
COULD IT REALLY BE?!
뚜벅
뚜벅
펄럭
IT'S BEEN A LONG TIME...
...PAMELA.

VIC....

...TOR...?!

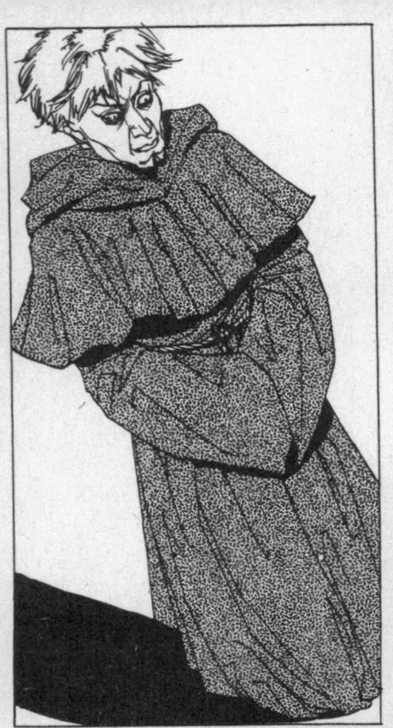

IT'S NICE TO MEET YOU, PAMELA.

I TOLD YOU WE'D BE SEEING EACH OTHER AGAIN.

AH, YOU HAVE COME.

YOU DON'T KNOW HOW LONG I'VE WAITED TO FIND SOMEONE LIKE YOU...

HAS THE PRINCESS GONE NIGHTY-NIGHT?

GET READY TO LIVE IN AN ENDLESS NIGHTMARE, PAMELA.
DRUNK WITH THE SCENT OF PERFUME...

ILLUSTRATION FROM THE HERBAL TAROT DECK.

*Nine of Pentacles: Right side up this card signifies material prosperity and the acquisition of wealth; superficiality. Upside down it signifies a threat to ownership of materials or the possibility of danger.

...LA...

...MELA...

다각
다각

TODAY IS THE DAY THEY HELP PEOPLE OUT AT THE ABBEY.
DIDN'T YOU KNOW THAT?

......

ISN'T IT NORMAL FOR DRAGONS TO WITHDRAW FROM THE WORLD TO AVOID HUMANS?

WHAT'S THE USE OF LIVING BY ONE'S SELF?
IT WOULD BE A BIT DANGEROUS, BUT I THINK IT WOULD BE BETTER TO LIVE AMONG OTHERS.

WHY DO I FEEL AS IF I'VE LIVED THROUGH SOMETHING LIKE THIS BEFORE?
다각다각
HUH?

THE NECKLACE IS ACTUALLY PERFUME THAT WILL BRING BACK YOUR MOST PAINFUL MEMORY OF THE PAST.
IT SEEMS THAT THINGS ARE GOING AS PLANNED.
WHEN YOU GO TO A PLACE OR MEET A PERSON THAT'S CONNECTED TO THIS MEMORY, YOU WILL BE TAKEN INTO A FANTASY WORLD THAT YOU CANNOT AWAKE FROM. OF ALL THE PERFUMES I'VE CREATED, THIS IS MY SECOND-MOST AMBITIOUS. HO HO...

I WONDER IF IT'S BECAUSE OF YOUR GOODNESS THAT I CAN ACHIEVE MY MOST ULTIMATE AMBITION.
WHAT'S SO GREAT ABOUT HER, ANYWAY? SHE'S WEAK, STUPID AND NOTHING SPECIAL TO LOOK AT.
IF ANYTHING BAD HAPPENS TO PAMELA, I'LL MAKE YOUR LIFE MISERABLE.

DAMN IT!

YOU HAVE A LOVE/HATE RELATIONSHIP WITH HER, I SEE.
MIND YOUR OWN BUSINESS.
SO, WHAT ARE YOU GOING TO DO TO HER? I ASSUME YOU HAVE SOME USE FOR HER.

I WAS BORN WITH A SENSE OF SMELL THAT'S A HUNDRED TIMES BETTER THAN OTHERS'...
BUT WITH THIS GIFT, THE GODS ALSO SENT A CURSE.

DO YOU THINK I'M REPULSIVE? WELL, EVEN I WEAR A MASK; I'M AFRAID TO LOOK IN THE MIRROR.
YOU LOOK LIKE AN OLD WOMAN, BUT I HEAR THAT YOU'RE ONLY IN YOUR 30S. IS THIS WHAT YOU MEAN?
YES, PREMATURE AGING. IT'S A DISEASE THAT AGES ME A LOT FASTER THAN OTHERS.
I LIKE BEAUTIFUL THINGS. THINGS THAT LOOK BEAUTIFUL, THINGS THAT SMELL BEAUTIFUL...THAT'S WHY I LIKE PERFUME.
BUT THERE'S NEVER BEEN A TIME WHERE I COULD WEAR A BEAUTIFUL SCENT, MYSELF.
I FOUND OUT A SURPRISING FACT ONE DAY, THOUGH.

IN THE 14TH CENTURY, QUEEN ELIZABETH OF HUNGARY WAS ABLE TO WOO THE KING OF POLAND BECAUSE OF A PARTICULAR PERFUME SHE WORE. SHE WAS OVER SEVENTY YEARS OLD.
UNFORTUNATELY, AS TIME WORE ON, THE SECRET OF HOW TO MAKE THE PERFUME WAS LOST.

YOU INTEND TO MAKE THE SAME PERFUME, DON'T YOU? THE ONE THE QUEEN WORE...
I WAS SUCCESSFUL IN MAKING IT BEFORE, OR SO I THOUGHT. ITS EFFECT TURNED OUT TO BE TEMPORARY, SO IT WAS A FAILURE.
IN ORDER TO MAKE IT WORK THIS TIME, I NEED THE LIFE-STRENGTH OF AN IMMORTAL BEING.
THE NAME OF THE PERFUME IS "QUEEN'S YOUTH." IT WILL BRING BACK LOST TIMES...

NECROMANCY ISN'T USED BY JUST ANYONE. NOT BY ANYONE BUT *YOU*, WHO'S REFERRED TO AS THE "QUEEN OF THE DEAD."

YOU USED HIM AT THE CHURCH INCIDENT TOO, DIDN'T YOU?

IT WAS A BIZARRE COINCIDENCE. TO THINK THAT HE WAS THE ONE THAT KILLED PAMELA'S LOVER...
MAYBE IT WASN'T A COINCIDENCE. HAS IT BEEN FIVE YEARS? HAVE YOU BEEN WELL?
YOU STILL HAVE A GIRLISH FACE.
ASH BECAME A HANDSOME YOUNG MAN. WHEN I LEFT, HE WAS JUST A KID WHO STILL SMELLED OF HIS MOTHER'S MILK.
WHY DID YOU LEAVE LIKE THAT?

TO HIM, YOU WERE FATHER, FRIEND, TEACHER... YOU WERE EVERYTHING.
ARE YOU ANGRY WITH ME? IS THAT WHY YOU WERE A PART OF ASH'S CRUELNESS? YOU'RE LIKE AN OVERPROTECTIVE MOTHER.

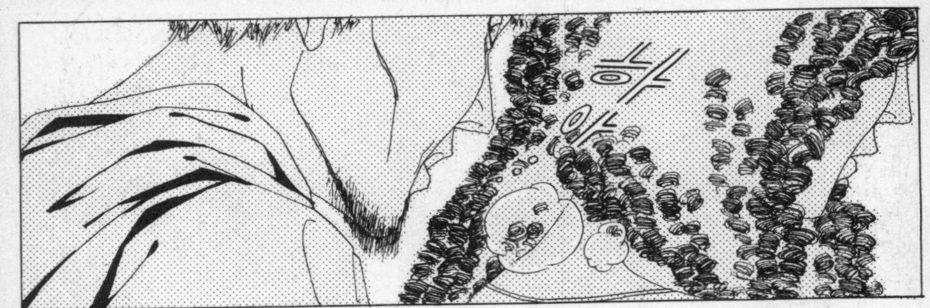
하아

깜짝

털썩

주섬 주섬
DO YOU HATE ME? I JUST WANTED TO SAY HELLO.

NO... YOU JUST STARTLED ME, SNEAKING UP BEHIND ME LIKE THAT.

OH...I'M SORRY. THEN...

THAT MONK IS CREEPY, PAMELA. WHENEVER YOU COME AROUND, HE HIDES FROM SIGHT AND GLARES AT YOU.
R-REALLY?

PAMELA, THERE'S AN INVALID IN TOWN I MUST SEE TO.
I'LL BE BACK TONIGHT. UNTIL THEN, CONTINUE TAKING CARE OF THE PEOPLE HERE.

WHAT? OH...OKAY.

I HAVE AN OMINOUS FEELING... BUT IT CAN'T BE REAL. IT'S JUST A FEELING, RIGHT?

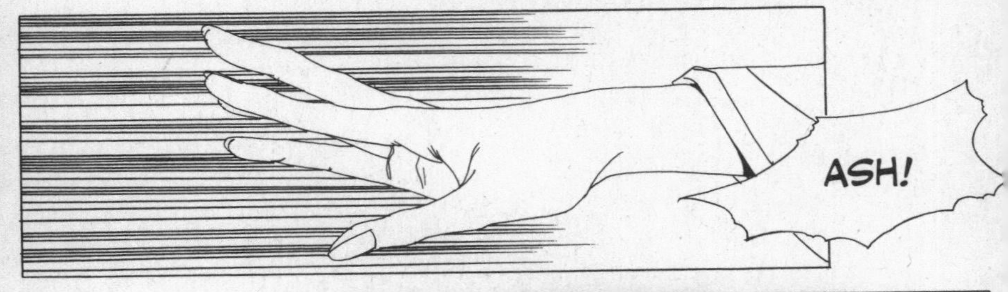

I HAVE A BAD FEELING ABOUT YOU GOING. PLEASE, STAY HERE...

IF I DON'T HELP HIM NOW, HE'LL DIE AND LEAVE HIS WIFE AND NINE CHILDREN WITH A VERY BLEAK FUTURE.

CAN YOU COME WITH ME TO THE CHAPEL FOR A MOMENT, PLEASE?
ASH ISN'T HERE...
I KNOW; IT'S YOU I NEED TO SPEAK WITH.

WHAT IS IT YOU NEED TO SPEAK WITH ME ABOUT?

FOR THE PAST THREE YEARS, WHENEVER I SEE YOU, MY HEART RACES!

I ADORE YOU. I WANT YOU TO BE MINE!
I'LL DO WHATEVER YOU SAY.

I'M SORRY, I'M IN LOVE WITH SOMEONE ELSE.

BESIDES, YOU'RE A MONK! YOU'RE SUPPOSED TO ADORE GOD, NOT ME.

THE PERSON YOU LOVE...DO YOU MEAN *HIM*?

WHY CAN'T YOU LOVE *ME*?

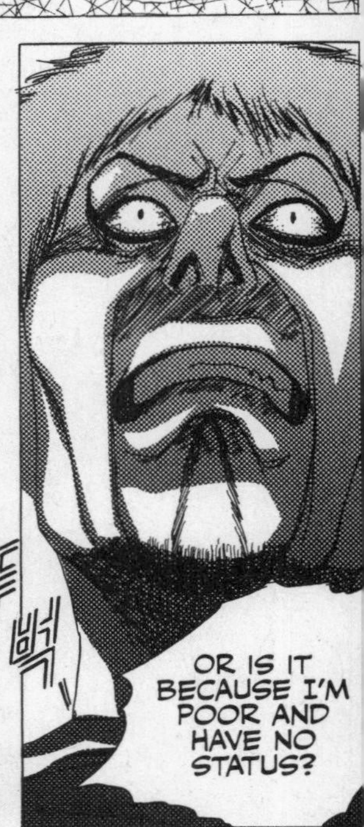

STOP BEING SO FOOLISH!
I LOVE ANOTHER, AND YOU ARE A MONK. THAT ALONE IS REASON ENOUGH!
I FIGURED YOU WOULD NEVER RETURN MY AFFECTION. THAT'S WHY I'VE NEVER TOLD YOU HOW I FEEL. I'VE ONLY WATCHED YOU...
AAAH!
BUT EVEN IF I HAVE TO SELL MY SOUL TO THE DEVIL, I WILL HAVE YOU AS MY OWN!

PLEASE... GET AWAY FROM ME!
IF I CAN'T HAVE YOU, NEITHER CAN HE! I'LL KILL YOU FIRST!
AAAH!
PLEASE! DON'T DO THIS, PLEASE!
PANT
PANT

AH!
STAY STILL!
OOF!
STOP RIGHT THERE!

UHH, UHH...
AHHH!
DID YOU MEAN WHAT YOU SAID BEFORE?

THAT YOU'D SELL YOUR SOUL TO THE DEVIL?
WHY, ARE YOU THE DEVIL OR SOMETHING?

I'LL MAKE ALL YOUR DESIRES A REALITY.

ILLUSTRATION FROM THE HERBAL TAROT DECK.

*Death: this card signifies that old things will pass and a new beginning will come.

ASH!
ASH!

WAH...
PAMELA.

ASH...?
HE WASN'T HERE A MINUTE AGO, WAS HE?
THE MONK WILL PAY FOR HIS SINS.
HE WILL NEVER REST...HE'LL BE STUCK IN AN EVER-TURNING WHEEL.
IF YOU KNEW ABOUT THE MONK, WHY DIDN'T YOU COME HELP ME?!
I WAS SO SCARED...
YOU HANDLED IT WELL ENOUGH ON YOUR OWN.

YOU CAN'T EXPECT ANYTHING FROM ME.
MY LIFE IS COMPLICATED ENOUGH WITH MY OWN PROBLEMS.

EVEN THE BEAUTY OF FLOWERS MEANS NOTHING TO ME.

TOO MUCH WEALTH IS WORSE THAN TOO LITTLE...

IF THE GROUND WAS COVERED WITH JEWELS INSTEAD OF PEBBLES, JEWELS WOULD HAVE NO VALUE.

IF ONLY I COULD EXPERIENCE THE BEATING OF MY OWN HEART AGAIN...

ALL THIS SOUNDS SO FAMILIAR...
PAMELA, LOVING YOU MORE THAN I LOVE MYSELF WOULD BE IMPOSSIBLE.

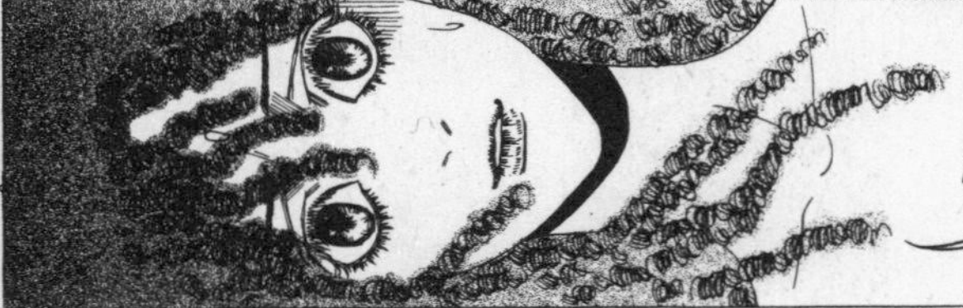
WHAT ARE YOU SAYING?
MY HEART HAS LIVED SO LONG THAT IT HAS PETRIFIED.
ASH?!

I'M SORRY.

THIS CAN'T BE REAL...

WHERE'S ASH?

WHY IS SHE LIKE THIS?
HAH, ARE YOU WORRIED THAT SOMETHING BAD IS GOING TO HAPPEN TO HER?

I'M ALMOST DONE...
YOU OLD COCOONED-FACED HAG!
DON'T TALK LIKE THAT...YOU'RE TAKING ALL THE FUN OUT OF THIS!

WHAT'S FUN ABOUT IT, ANYWAY?
THE INGREDIENT I NEED FOR THE PERFUME IS NOT EASY TO EXTRACT...I HAVE TO TRY AGAIN.
UHHH...
PAMELA.
WONDERING WHY YOU'RE HERE?

YOU'RE BEING PUNISHED.

BAD GIRLS WHO STEAL OTHERS' PRECIOUS BELONGINGS MUST BE PUNISHED.

HEY! ARE YOU OKAY?

GROAN...

ARE YOU HURT?

NO INGREDIENT COMPARES TO THE SCENT OF A WOMAN WHO ATTRACTS THE OPPOSITE SEX!

HO HO...
NOW I ONLY HAVE THREE MORE PEOPLE'S SCENTS TO COLLECT.

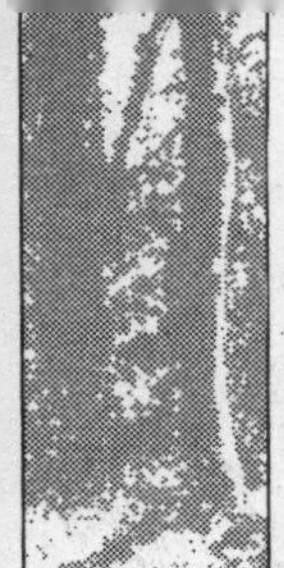

다각
다각

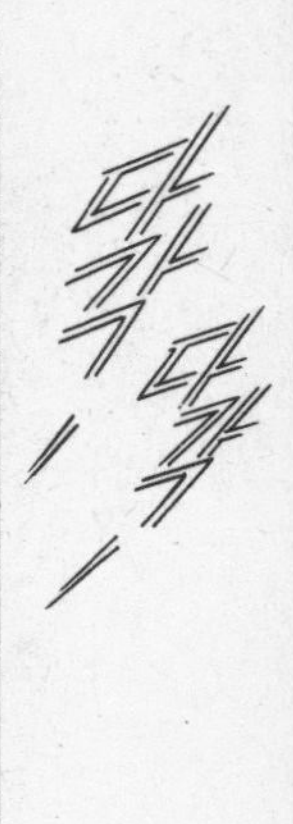

다각
다각

I'M BERIAL, THE KING OF DECEIT AND EVIL.
YOUR DESIRES GUIDE MY WAY IN HELL.

HAH HAH HAH...
KING OF HELL...YOUR FRIENDSHIP WOULD SUIT ME VERY WELL.

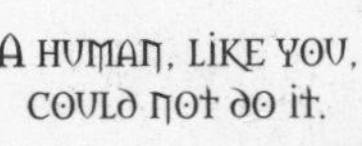

DO YOU WISH TO BE RID OF THE ONE WHO POSSESSES PAMELA?
HE'S AN IMMORTAL BEING, YOU KNOW.
A HUMAN, LIKE YOU, COULD NOT DO IT.

How good would it feel to have her forever, as an immortal?

I can lend you that kind of strength, if you desire it.

척척척척
척척척척척
탁탁탁

IT WILL BEAR FRUIT, BUT WHETHER IT WILL BE POISONOUS OR SWEET...

DON'T TRUST EVERYTHING THAT YOU SEE. DON'T TRUST ANYONE.

IT JUST DOESN'T FEEL RIGHT...

멈칫

WHAT WAS THAT?

SOMETHING DOESN'T FEEL RIGHT...

PAMELA...
ARE YOU ASH'S SYLPH?
WHERE'S ASH?
HE'S AT THE RUINS AT THE SOUTHERN END OF TOWN, BUT A STRANGE POWER IS KEEPING ME FROM HIM.
RUINS? HE SAID HE WAS GOING TO SEE A PATIENT...
GO TO ALECTO AND ASK FOR HIS HELP. SOMETHING IS VERY WRONG.

YES, ALECTO'S A JERK, BUT HE'S THE ONLY ONE I CAN ASK FOR HELP....
척척척척

I'M THE MESSENGER WHO, IN THE NAME OF GOD, JUDGED THE DEVIL'S PERPETRATOR!

I WAS TIMID IN THE PRESENCE OF YOUR SHINING BEAUTY.

AND STILL YOUR BEAUTY MAKES MY HEART BEAT FAST.

THE ONE WHO HAS A CONTRACT WITH THE DEVIL IS GOING TO JUDGE HIS PERPETRATOR?
THAT'S A LAUGH.

BUT IT'S THE FATE OF YOUR BEAUTY TO BE DESTROYED.
SHUT UP! I KNOW THAT YOU ARE A DRAGON, AN ENEMY OF OUR GOD! IT WOULD BE BEST TO WILLINGLY GIVE UP YOUR LIFE NOW.
WHAT DO YOU WANT, *APPLAUSE*?
YOU HAVE A CONTRACT WITH A HIGH-RANKING DEVIL.
I KNOW OF ONLY THREE WITH THE ABILITY TO MAKE A COMMON MONK INTO A BISHOP WITH THIS LARGE ARMY AND THAT KNOW THE DRAGON SLAYER SPELL.
HELLO, BERIAL.
IT'S GOOD TO SEE YOU TOO, ASH. YOU CAN THANK PAMELA FOR US BEING ABLE TO MEET AGAIN.

FIRE!

FIRE!

IS IT MY TURN YET?
AAAAAH!

I SEE THAT YOU WILL NOT DIE WITHOUT A FIGHT. WELL, THINGS WILL WORK OUT WHEN THE STAR OF THE SHOW COMES OUT.
PAMELA!
SHE'S THE WITCH WHO SIDES WITH THE DRAGON! AIM FOR HER!
ASH!

F-I-R-E-!

IF I CAN'T HAVE YOU, I'LL DESTROY YOU, PAMELA.

YES... I HAVE SEEN THIS SPECTACLE BEFORE.

AND...

AND...

ILLUSTRATION FROM THE HERBAL TAROT DECK.

*Strength: This card represents the physical and mental courage that does not yield to outward pressure; one who takes action.

LONG AGO, WHEN THE WORLD OF FANTASY AND REALITY WERE STILL INTERTWINED...
A DRAGON AND A GIRL LOVED EACH OTHER.
...AT LEAST, THAT'S WHAT THE GIRL BELIEVED TO BE SO.

ALL ALONE, THE GIRL BEGAN A LONG JOURNEY TO FIND THE DRAGON.

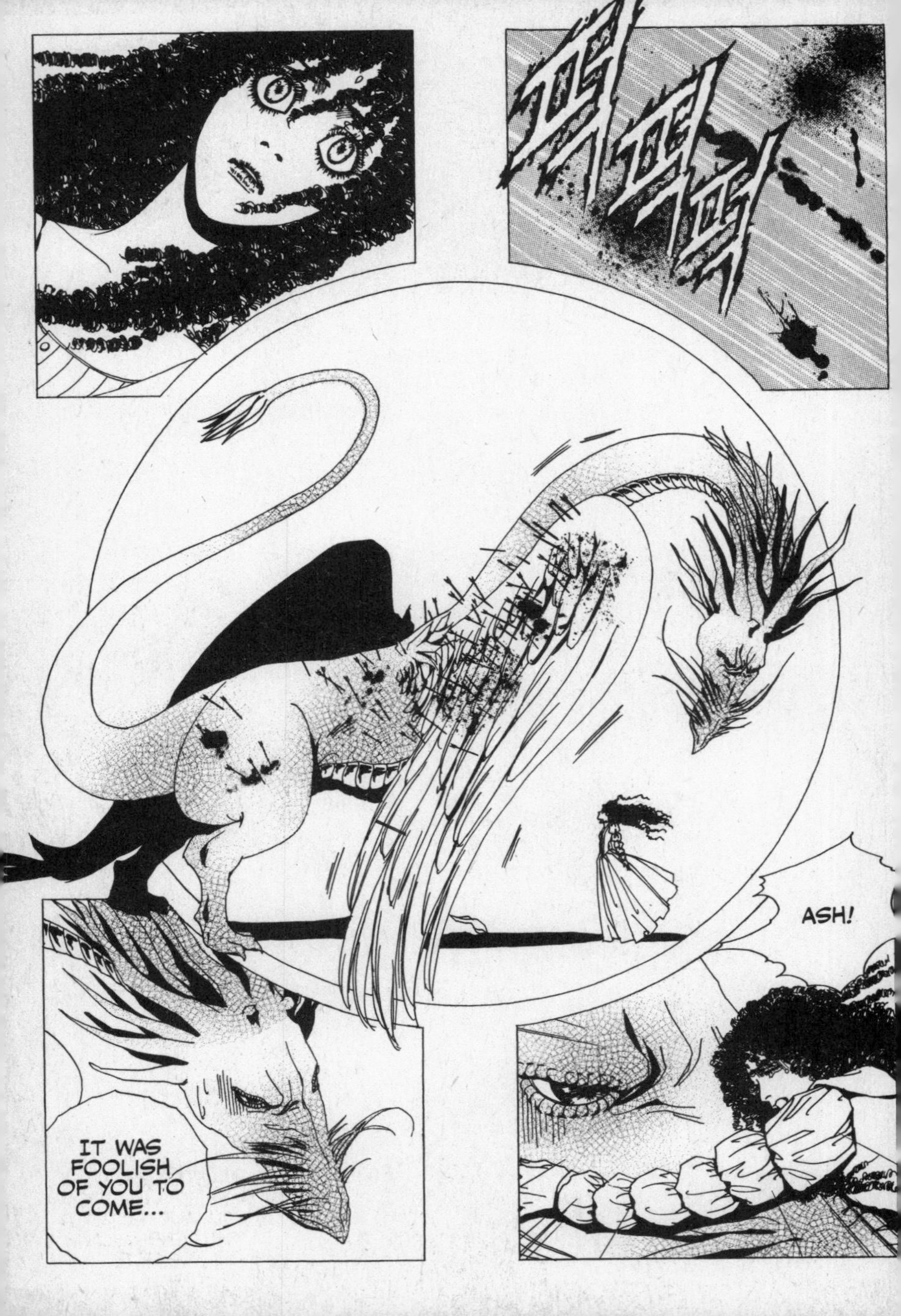

ASH!
IT WAS FOOLISH OF YOU TO COME...

I'M SORRY. I KNEW THAT YOU WENT TO THE MONASTERY, BUT I DIDN'T KNOW *THAT*.

WHY DIDN'T YOU TELL ME BEFORE?

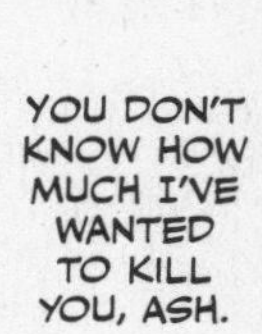

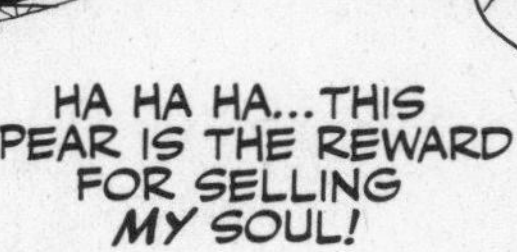

THAT'S RIGHT! I REMEMBER...
FOR HUNDREDS OF YEARS I WAS ABLE TO FORGET THIS NIGHTMARE...

ALL OF THIS...

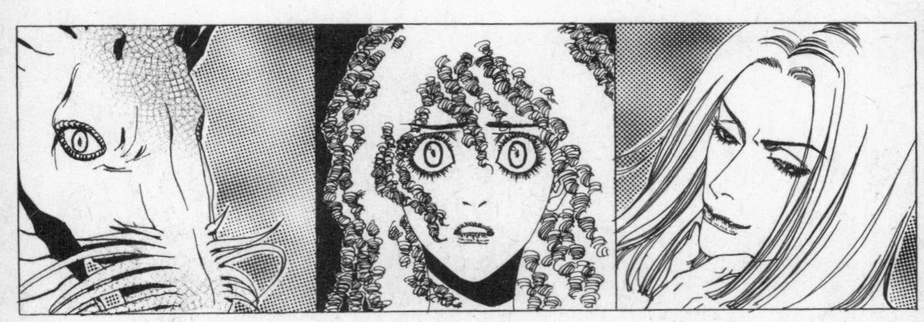

HOW AM I RELIVING IT AGAIN?
AM I DREAMING?
ASH!
DID I RETURN TO THE PAST?

NOW, JUST A LITTLE BIT MORE...
...A LITTLE MORE...
탁
IT'S FINALLY COMPLETE! I'M DONE!

CONGRATULATIONS. I'M STILL CURIOUS ABOUT SOMETHING, THOUGH:
EARLIER, WHEN YOU MET PAMELA ON THE TRAIN--YOU HAD A YOUTHFUL FACE. HOW DID YOU MANAGE THAT ONE?
I SPRAYED THIS ON.
WHAT YOU SAW WAS WHAT I WANTED TO LOOK LIKE. AND NOW IT CAN BE A REALITY.
QUEEN'S YOUTH IS A PERFUME THAT CAN TRULY GIVE ME YOUTH. NO MORE ILLUSIONS ARE NEEDED!
I HAVE WAITED SO LONG FOR THIS DAY...
YOU MUST BE ECSTATIC.

I DON'T HAVE TO LIVE WITH A MASK ANY LONGER!

YOU NO LONGER HAVE TO *LIVE* AT ALL...
YOU'LL DIE EVENTUALLY ANYWAY.
!!
AAAH!

I REPLACED ONE OF YOUR PRECIOUS INGREDIENTS WITH POISON.
I SO WANTED TO BE BEAUTIFUL... EVEN FOR JUST ONE MOMENT...
EVEN FOR JUST ONE MOMENT...

HMM, I GUESS CORA TOLD YOU.
YOU'RE TOO LATE, ANYWAY.

YOU ARE AN UNDISCIPLINED CHILD.
HAH!
NOW PAMELA MUST RELIVE THE MOST PAINFUL EXPERIENCE OF HER LIFE OVER AND OVER AGAIN.
TELL ME HOW TO WAKE HER UP!
SHE CANNOT AWAKEN WITHOUT TASTING THE BLOOD FROM SOMEONE'S HEART.
IN OTHER WORDS, SOMEONE MUST DIE TO SAVE HER. DO YOU LOVE HER THAT MUCH?

HAH HAH HAH...
DI...DIE...
JUST DIE!
?!!
?

ASH...

I'M SORRY...
ASH...?

HAH HAH HAH!
NO, THIS ISN'T REAL...
IT'S JUST AN ILLUSION...
AAAH!
ILLUSION OR NOT, THOUGH...

I'VE WANTED TO KILL YOU, VICTOR!
I'VE IMAGINED KILLING YOU A COUNTLESS NUMBER OF TIMES, EVERY DAY FOR HUNDREDS OF YEARS.
DIE...
JUST DIE!

ARE YOU BACK?

I'VE BEEN WAITING FOR YOU.

BELUS!
BEL...

CAFE
TAROT

THE MOON COVERED BY CLOUDS WILL REAPPEAR AND SHED LIGHT ON THE TRUTH...

KNIGHT OF SWORDS
THE ONE NEAR THE CORE OF AN ISSUE WILL UNTIE THE KNOT FROM THE MIDDLE.

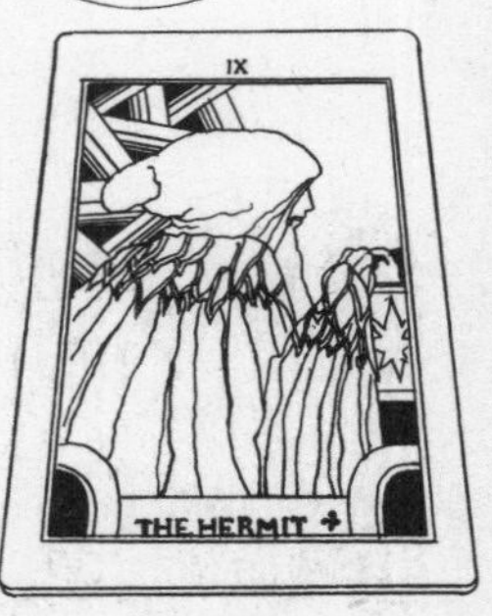
THE ONE WHO WILL GIVE ME INSPIRATION WILL APPEAR?
IX
THE HERMIT

HMM...

WHAT ARE YOU THINKING ABOUT?

ALTHOUGH MY JOURNEY TO SCOTLAND WAS TERRIBLE, I FEEL LIKE I CAME BACK WITH SOMETHING VALUABLE.

WELL, JUST THIS AND THAT.
HOW DO YOU FEEL? SINCE YOU'RE WALKING AROUND, I'M GUESSING YOU'RE OKAY.

WHAT HAPPENED TO VICTOR?

I KNOW HE WASN'T AN ILLUSION!

AAAH!

WHY DID YOU INTERFERE?

YOUR THOUGHTS WERE SENT TO HIM. I THOUGHT THAT WAS ENOUGH.

I MAKE THE DECISIONS. YOU DO WHAT I TELL YOU TO DO.
PRETENTIOUS BRAT...

PANT
PANT

HUFF
PANT
HUFF
탁탁탁
털썩
!!!

KING OF RODS

ILLUSTRATION FROM MORGAN-GREER TAROT.

Tree and Long-Horned Beetle

*King of Rods: Right-side up this card signifies an honest, conscientious, diligent, and noble person. Upside down it signifies a strict, but diligently reserved person.

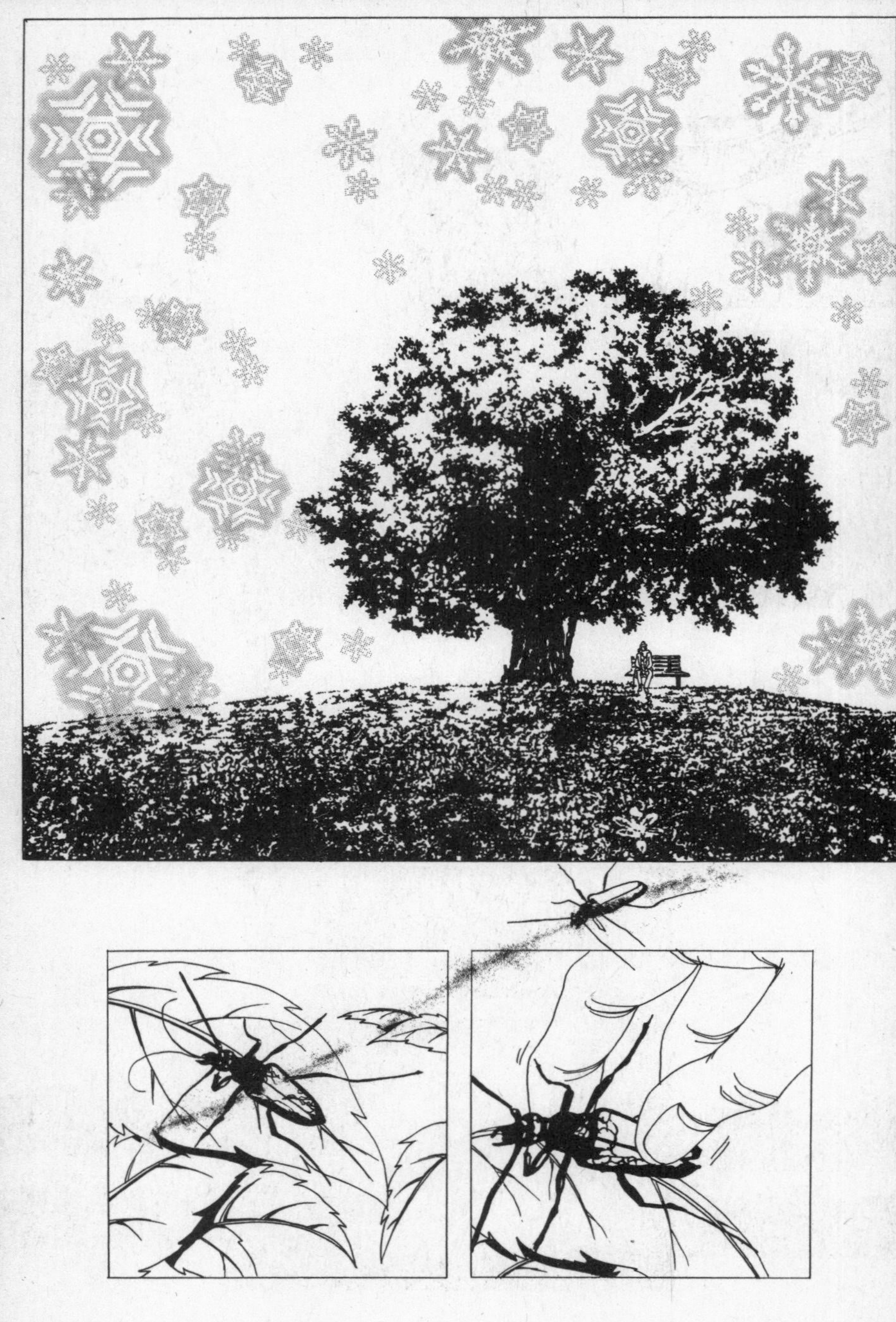

DO YOU NEED SOME HELP?

SEEK OUT A WOMAN NAMED PAMELA. SHE WILL HELP YOU.

CAFE
TAROT
NEW OPEN
CENTRAAL
Spring 1995

WOW! IS THIS STRAWBERRY PIE?!
LOOKS DELICIOUS...
WOW, PAMELA CAN COOK, TOO?
HO HO, WHAT *CAN'T* I DO? I'M JUST TOO LAZY TO DO IT VERY OFTEN.
PAMELA'S WON AWARDS FOR HER PIES.

WHAT CONTEST WAS IT? "WHICH COUNTRY MAID CAN MAKE THE TASTIEST PIE"?
AT THAT TIME, PAMELA WAS 500 YEARS OLD AND STILL SINGLE.
OH MY GOSH! ARE YOU OKAY?!
URGH. YOU JUST HIT ME WHERE I WAS STABBED BEFORE...
I'M OKAY. I WAS JUST PLAYING AROUND.

LET ME SEE.
I SAID IT'S OKAY!
UGH!
WELL, I SAID LET ME TAKE A LOOK!
WHY ARE YOU DOING THIS?
HOW CAN BELUS HAVE A SCAR?
I THINK THIS IS THE FIRST TIME...
I SAID IT'S OKAY!

YOU TWO ARE ACTING ALL WEIRD AROUND EACH OTHER SINCE WHAT HAPPENED IN SCOTLAND.

WHAT DO YOU MEAN?
IT MAY NOT SEEM LIKE IT, BUT I'M VERY PERCEPTIVE.

THERE'S SOME OLD GRANDPA STARING AT US OUT THERE.

YOU MUST BE COLD. CARE TO WARM UP WITH SOME TEA?
쪼르륵
HMM! I DON'T NEED ANY TEA!
BUT SINCE YOU ASKED SO NICELY...
WOULD YOU LIKE ME TO READ YOUR FORTUNE?
OUCH, IT'S HOT! I CAN'T BELIEVE YOU WOULD GIVE AN OLD MAN SUCH A THING!
CAN YOU TELL ME THIS BOY'S FUTURE?

FUTURE IS THE PRODUCT OF THE PAST AND THE PRESENT.
SO I SHOULD LOOK INTO HIS PAST, TOO.
LET'S SEE...

THE TOWER: Upside down this card can represent tyranny; something that endangers one's freedom. Right side up it can mean something that weakens one's power.

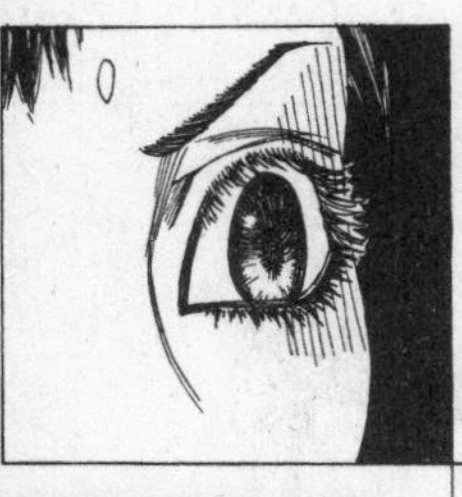

WHO IS THIS CHILD?!

HE IS MY ONE AND ONLY FRIEND. I MET HIM TWO YEARS AGO.

쿵쿵
IT'S MY FAULT...

쿵쿵
IT'S ALL MY FAULT.

쿵쿵
IT'S ALL MY FAULT.

WHY ARE YOU BANGING YOUR HEAD ON THIS TREE? I SUSPECT IT'S MORE THAN JUST YOUR HEAD THAT IS HURTING.

WAH!
YIKES!

WHERE DO YOU LIVE?
WHY WERE YOU DOING THAT?

WHERE IS YOUR MOTHER?

...?
I DON'T HAVE A MOTHER ANYMORE.
SHE SAID SHE COULD NO LONGER LIVE WITH ME BECAUSE I BROUGHT HER BAD LUCK.
HMM! ALL HUMAN BEINGS ARE BAD LUCK. THEY CUT DOWN TREES AND POLLUTE THE AIR AND WATER.

AFTER THAT, THE BOY CAME TO SEE ME OFTEN.

DO YOU KNOW THIS PLACE WELL?

YES. THIS TREE, THIS HILL, AND THE CLOUDS...

A LOT OF LONG-HORNED BEETLES LIVE IN THIS TREE. TREES WITH THESE BEETLES HAVE LOTS OF FLOWERS GROWING ON THEM.

I DON'T LIKE BUGS VERY MUCH.

SO...ALL OF SUDDEN, I STARTED TO WAIT FOR THE LITTLE BOY.

WERE YOU WAITING FOR ME?

I JUST CAME OUT TO TAKE A STROLL.

WHAT ARE THOSE WOUNDS?
YOU ALWAYS HAVE MARKS ON YOUR BODY.

OH, I... FALL A LOT.

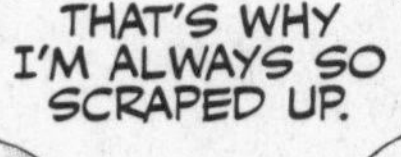
THAT'S WHY I'M ALWAYS SO SCRAPED UP.

......

YEP, THAT'S RIGHT.

부스럭
THEY WERE GIVING FOOD AWAY AT CHURCH, AND THEY GAVE ME TWO.
THE PASTOR SAID THAT I SHOULD SHARE ONE WITH A FRIEND.

HERE...

I DON'T LIKE THINGS LIKE THAT VERY MUCH.

우물우물
BUT THERE ARE TIMES I WANT TO EAT THEM.
A FRIEND...

YOU AND YOUR GRANDSON SEEM TO HAVE A GOOD RELATIONSHIP.

I TOOK A PICTURE BECAUSE YOU TWO LOOKED VERY HAPPY. THAT'LL BE $2.50.

I DON'T HAVE ANY MONEY!

THE PICTURE CAME OUT NICELY, DON'T YOU THINK?

I'D LIKE TO TAKE SOME OF THIS PIE TO THE BOY.

FIVE OF PENTACLES: This card represents being without the basic ingredients of life, such as love, shelter, food, etc.; loneliness.

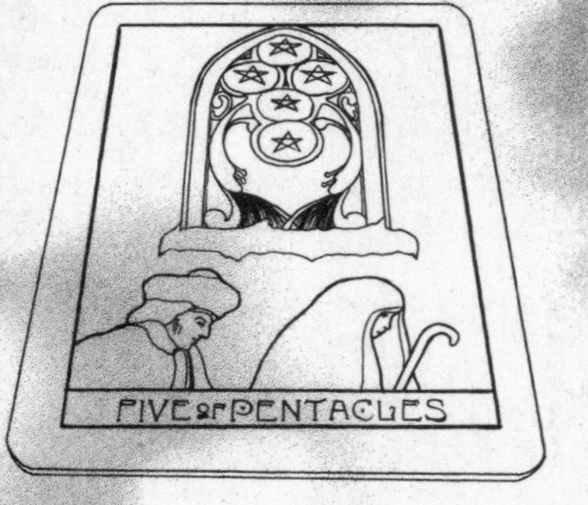

CLOTHES BANK
SCOPE

WHAT ARE YOU LOOKING AT?!

HM! HE LOOKS AT YOU WITH CONTEMPT LIKE HIS MOTHER USED TO. HOW DARE YOU LOOK AWAY WHEN AN ADULT IS SPEAKING TO YOU?!
YOU BASTARD! I *ASKED* WHAT YOU WERE LOOKING AT! HOW DARE YOU LOOK AWAY FROM ME WHEN I'M SPEAKING TO YOU!
YOU LITTLE PUKE.
THAT'S HOW HE GOT ALL THE WOUNDS ON HIS BODY.
FATHER! I'M SORRY!
AAAH!
AAAH!
AAAH! AAAH!
BUT...

DAMN, DID HE KICK THE BUCKET?

HEY, WE'RE OUT OF BEER. YOU WANNA GO DRINK AT MY HOUSE?

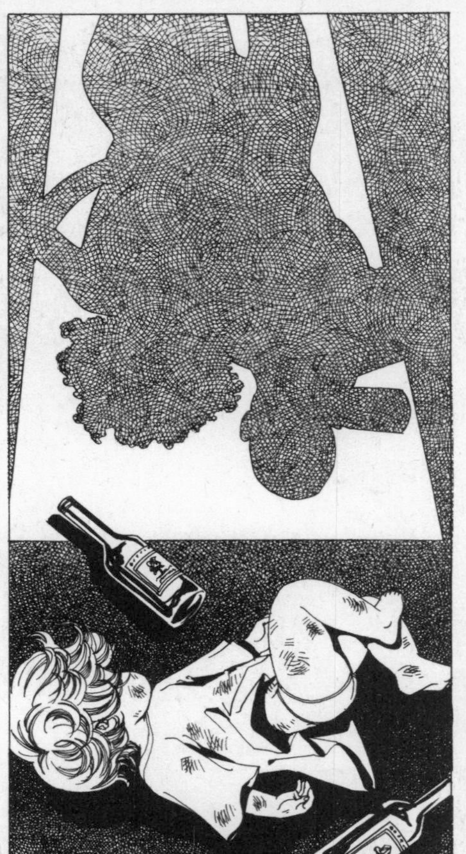

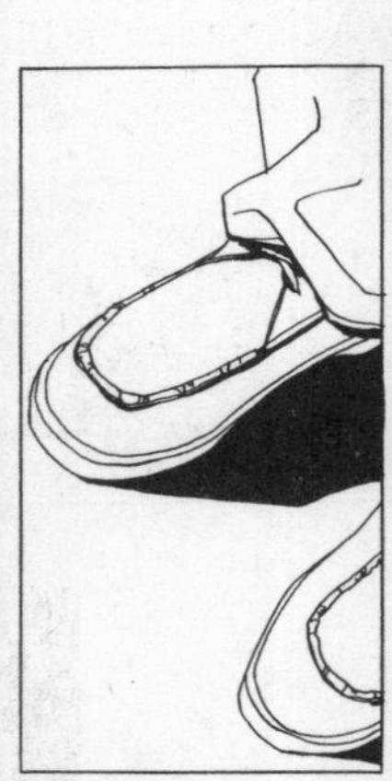

IT WAS STRANGE...HE NEVER SKIPPED A SINGLE DAY, AND THEN SUDDENLY HE DIDN'T SHOW UP AT ALL.

I HAD NOT BEEN TO WHERE THE HUMANS LIVED FOR MANY YEARS, BUT I WAS CURIOUS ABOUT WHAT HAPPENED TO THE BOY.

LITTLE BOY, ARE YOU HERE?

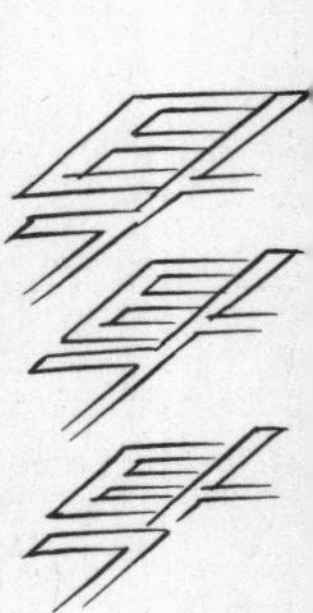

HE WAS BROUGHT IN WITH PERITONITIS AND RUPTURED INTERNAL ORGANS. HE HAD BEEN IN THAT CONDITION FOR SEVERAL DAYS WHEN WE FIRST SAW HIM...IT'S A MIRACLE HE WAS EVEN ALIVE.

ARE YOU HIS GUARDIAN?

HOW IS HE?

HE HAS TO UNDERGO SURGERY SOON. IF WE WAIT MUCH LONGER, THERE WILL BE NO HOPE FOR HIM.

IN ALL THE HUNDREDS OF YEARS I'VE BEEN ALIVE, HE'S THE FIRST FRIEND I'VE HAD.

THIS IS THE ONLY THING I CAN DO FOR HIM.

KNIGHT OF PENTACLES: This card represents a man with a great sense of responsibility, patience, usefulness, and service.

THANK YOU.
I'LL BE GOING THEN...
WAIT! WHAT ABOUT MY FEE?!
TAKE A LONG LOOK AT MY BACKSIDE! YOU WILL PROBABLY RECOGNIZE IT AFTER DOING WHAT I ASKED YOU TO DO.

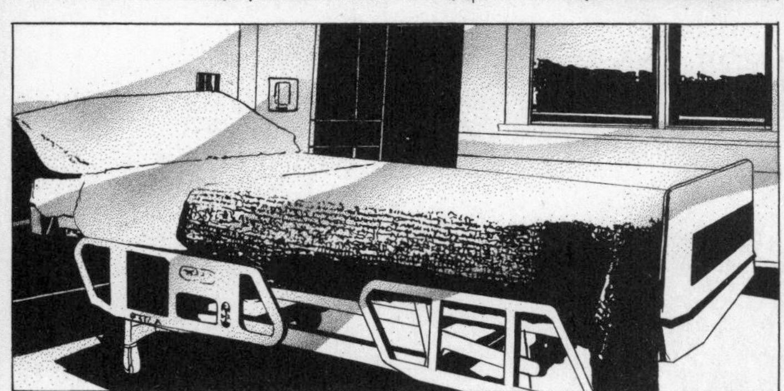

FATHER... YOU'RE HURTING ME...
PLEASE...TAKE ME... TO THE HOSPITAL...
FATHER...

YOU IDIOT! SHUT UP!
I DON'T HAVE THE MONEY TO TAKE YOU TO A DOCTOR THIS TIME!
I HAVE DEBT UP TO MY NECK BECAUSE OF THE BAD LUCK YOU BRING ME!

IT WOULD BE BETTER IF YOU JUST DISAPPEARED LIKE YOUR MOTHER DID!

AH, THAT'S GOOD!

PANT
PANT
PANT
PANT

PANT

PANT

PANT

PANT

PANT

CAN'T YOU SHUT HIM UP?

ALL THAT PANTING WEIRDS ME OUT.

IF I HURT YOU IN ANOTHER SPOT, YOU'LL FEEL FINE EVERYWHERE ELSE. HAH HAH HAH...

AAAH!!

WHO'S THERE?!
HE SAID HE WAS HURTING... I TRIED TO HELP HIM.
WHAT DO YOU CARE WHAT I DO WITH MY SON, ANYWAY?
ARE YOU THE ONE WHO HARMED THIS BOY?

HEY! THAT'S MY SON! PUT HIM DOWN!

HEY, OLD MAN! I'M GOING TO KILL YOU!

WHAT?

WHAT, WHAT *IS* THAT?!

I HAVE
A FAVOR
TO ASK
OF YOU.

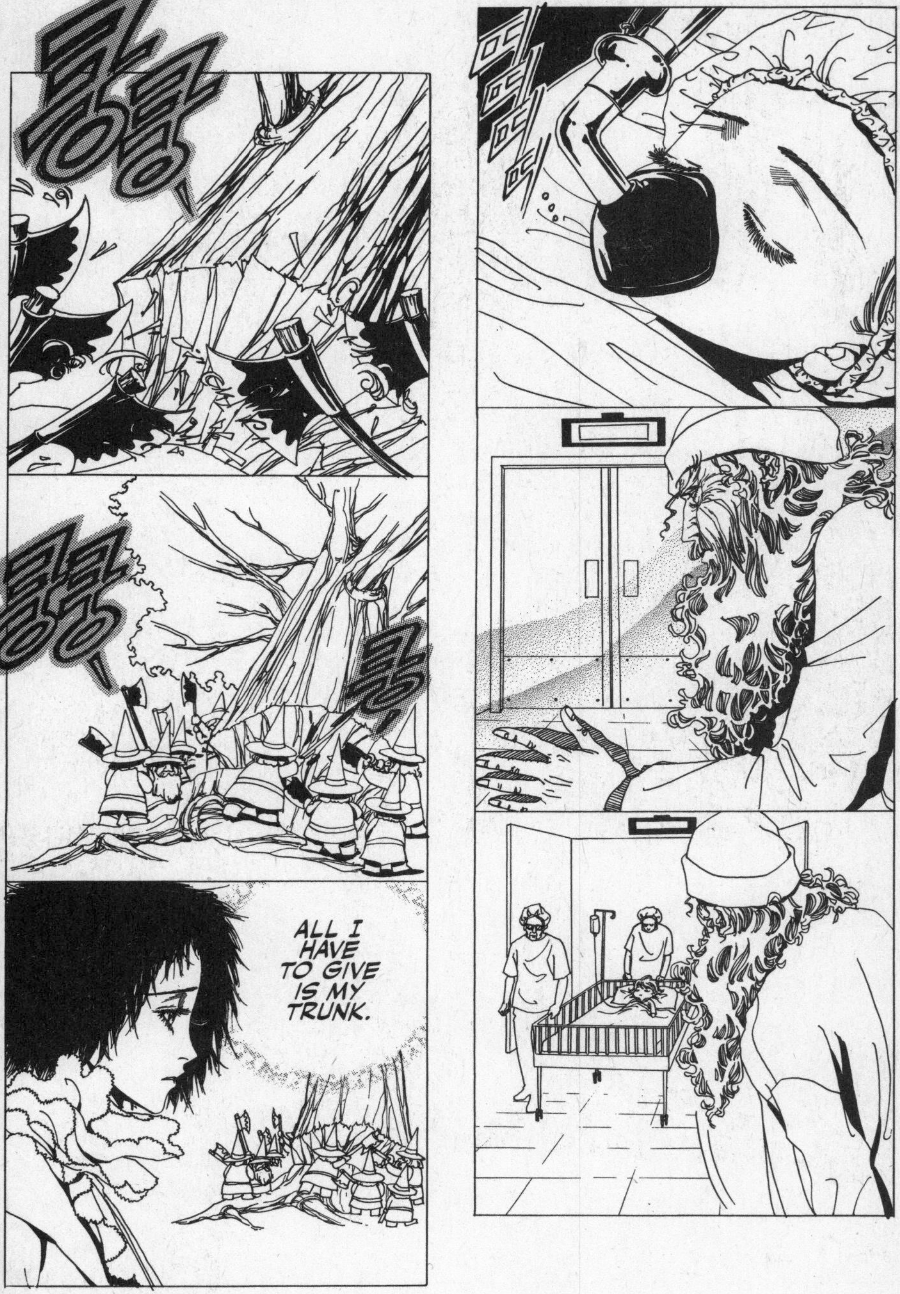

ALL I HAVE TO GIVE IS MY TRUNK.

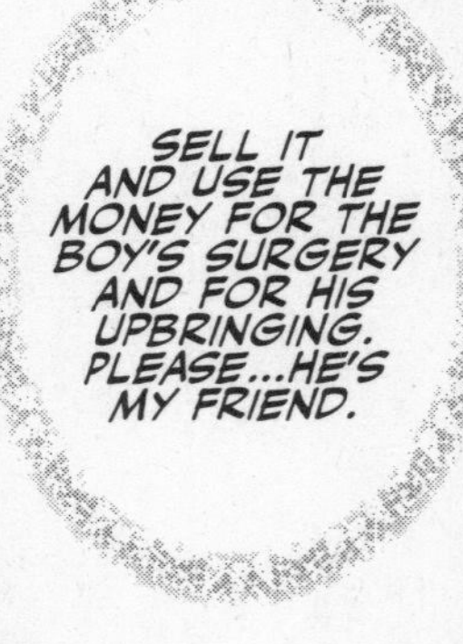

SELL IT AND USE THE MONEY FOR THE BOY'S SURGERY AND FOR HIS UPBRINGING. PLEASE...HE'S MY FRIEND.

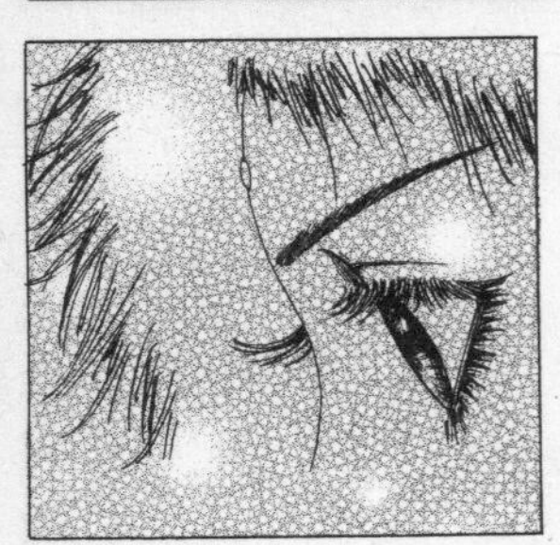

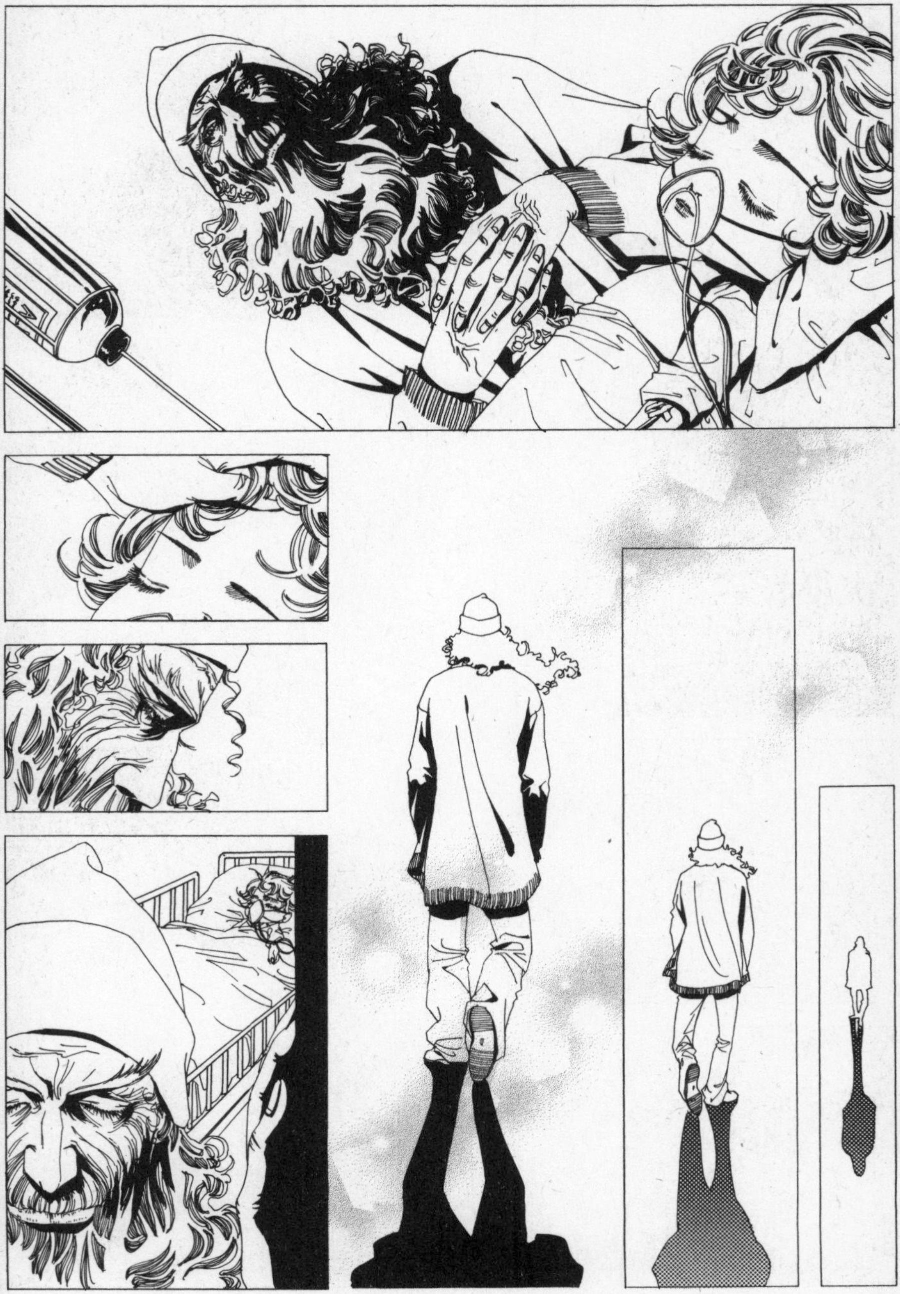

A LOT OF LONG-HORNED BEETLES LIVED IN THIS TREE. I HEARD THAT TREES WITH LONG-HORNED BEETLES LIVING IN THEM HAVE LOTS OF FLOWERS.

YES. THIS TREE, THIS HILL AND THE CLOUDS...

I DON'T LIKE BUGS VERY MUCH.

BUT I THINK THE LONG-HORNED BEETLES ARE OKAY.

YEAH?

IX CONTEMPLATION

Episode 17: Invitation to hell

CHANG O

MEANING OF THE CARD: The need to go within to gain knowledge to one's own divinity. Withdrawal to better contemplate life. Upside down, it represents distracted by the world, refusal to listen to intuition, no time to think or reflect.

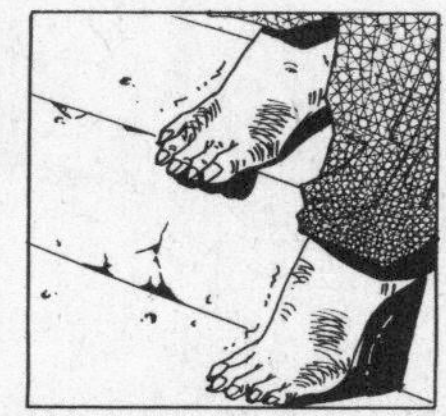

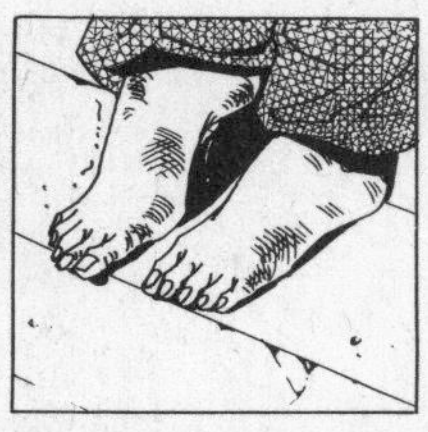

끼이익

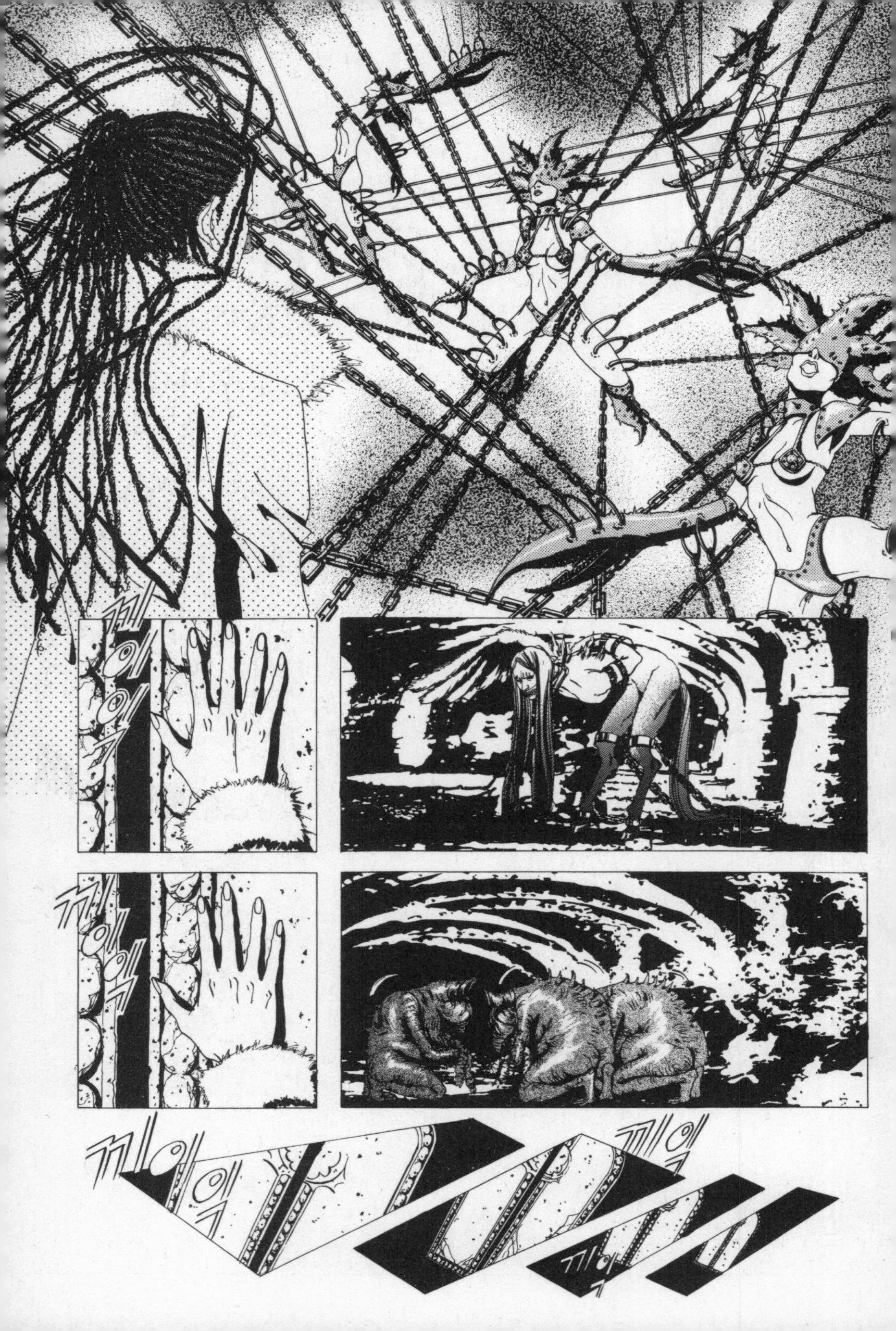

끼이익
끼이익
끼이익
끼익
끼익

끼익
!!!

YOU SURVIVED THE JAWS OF DEATH.

WHAT KIND OF PLACE IS THIS? WHO COULD HAVE AFFLICTED SUCH HARM ON YOU?

THE REASON YOU'RE HERE... HAVE YOU COME SEEKING THE TRUTH?

THE PLACE I WENT WAS HELL...
IT WAS THE DEEPEST, DARKEST ABYSS OF ALL HELLS.
THE GREAT EMPEROR OF HELL'S DOMAIN... BERIAL'S CASTLE!!!

CAFE
TAROT
Spring 1995

달칵
파앗

THEY SAY THAT ONCE A YEAR, THE GREAT SAGE COMES TO TOWN.
PEOPLE RECEIVE HIS BREAD, GET TREATED FOR SICKNESS, OR ASK ABOUT THEIR FUTURE.
LOOK-- HE'S OVER THERE. WE SHOULD HAVE SOME BREAD, TOO.
DO YOU BELIEVE IN SALVATION?
DOES THE GOD YOU BELIEVE IN REALLY EXIST?

IT'S MERELY AN APPEALING FABLE, MADE UP BY THE STRONG TO REGULATE THE WEAK.

DID YOUR GOD EVER GIVE YOU BREAD?

NO-- WHEN YOU ARE MOANING IN PAIN, HE DOESN'T HELP YOU! HE DOESN'T EXIST!

LITTLE CHILD...
COME, HAVE SOME BREAD.

I CAN SEE YOUR TRUE FORM...
AND IT'S DIRTY, VILE AND DISTORTED.

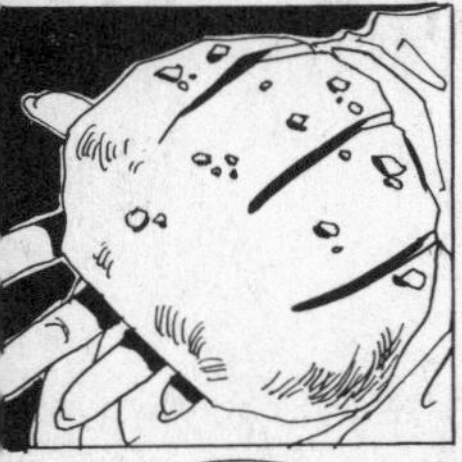

YOU'RE NO SAGE.

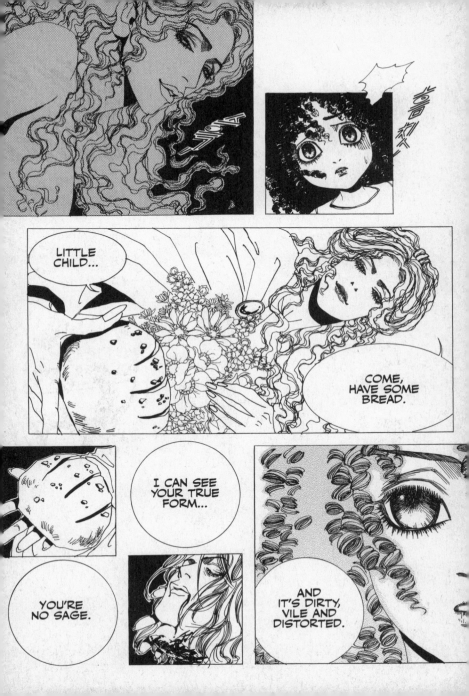

?!!
WHAT AN ADORABLE CHILD. WHAT'S YOUR NAME?
PAMELA.
NO HUMAN HAS EVER BEEN ABLE TO SEE THROUGH ME BEFORE.
YOU AMUSE ME, PAMELA.

I APOLOGIZE... SHE'S YOUNG...
WE'LL BE SEEING EACH OTHER AGAIN, PAMELA.
THAT MAN... WHO IS HE?
I'VE SEEN HIM BEFORE...

STAY STILL FOR A MOMENT.
W-WHAT?

WHAT ARE YOU DOING-- IT'S DARK IN HERE! AREN'T YOU SUPPOSED TO BE RUNNING A BUSINESS?

I HAVE TO BE GOING NOW...

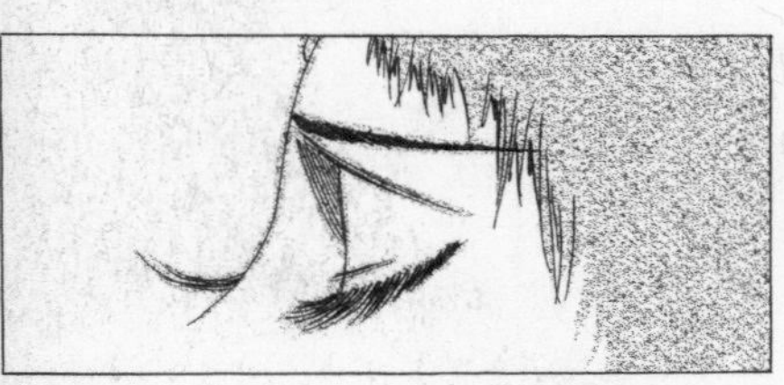

ELIZABETH·II D·G·REG·F·D

WHAT ARE YOU DOING?

TA-DA! IT'S A MAGIC TRICK I FOUND ON THE INTERNET. PRETTY AMAZING, HUH?

WHAT DO YOU MEAN *AMAZING*? YOU DORK!

I'LL TELL YOU WHAT'S AMAZING: PART OF MY MEMORY NO LONGER EXISTS.

WHAT?

I THINK SOMEONE HAS ERASED MY MEMORY.

BERIAL'S HOBBY IS TO COLLECT RARE ORGANISMS.

WHETHER THEY'RE ALIVE OR DEAD...IT DOESN'T MATTER.

THAT'S PROBABLY WHY I'M HERE AT HIS CASTLE--I'M PART OF HIS COLLECTION.

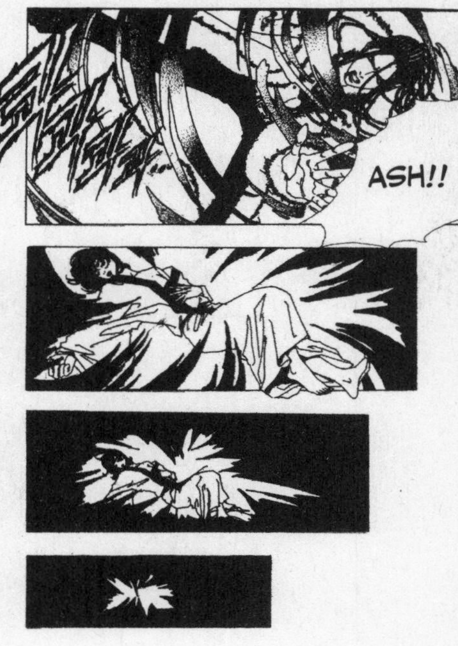

I WAS DRAGGED TO HIS CASTLE, LIKE A BUTTERFLY SPECIMEN THAT HAD NOT QUITE DIED.
I DON'T REMEMBER *HOW* I ESCAPED. IT'S ALL VERY UNCLEAR.
I WAS UNABLE TO MOVE AT ALL.
I WAS JUST LOOKING FOR AN EXIT...

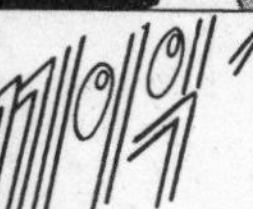
끼이익

스윽

HEH, HEH, HEH... I'VE BEEN WAITING FOR YOU, ALECTO.

ARE YOU THE OLD FORTUNE READER I MET LONG AGO...?

HEH, HEH, HEH...IT'S BEEN A WHILE, ALECTO. I'VE BEEN WAITING TO TELL YOU THE TRUTH.

THE TRUTH?

THE DEVIL: This card is symbolic for what is bad and undesirable. It refers to one staying in ignorance, remaining in bondage, and feeling hopelessness and despair.

THE

WHAT'S GOING ON RIGHT NOW IS A GAME OF DECEPTION.

AND THOSE WHO PLAY THE GAME ARE MERE PAWNS WITHIN IT.

YOU ARE DECEIVING YOURSELF.
BECAUSE OF YOUR PRIDE, YOU TURN AWAY FROM YOUR TRUE FEELINGS. YOU TURN AWAY FROM YOURSELF.

Eight of Swords: this card stands for those times when we feel help is out of reach. It refers to one feeling victimized, trapped by circumstances, and being unsure of which way to turn for guidance and clarity.

YOU JUST DON'T WANT TO ACKNOWLEDGE IT.
WHAT?!!
IT'S FUNNY--YOUR COMPANION DOESN'T EVEN RECOGNIZE YOU. HE'S NOT EVEN INTERESTED IN YOU.
YOU HAVE NEVER BEEN ABLE TO GET CLOSE TO THE TRUTH. YOU HAVE ONLY CIRCLED AROUND IT.
SECRETLY, THOUGH, YOU HAVE STOLEN GLANCES AT IT.
SO, ALTHOUGH YOU DON'T REALIZE IT, YOU *HAVE* SEEN TRUTH.
DO YOU REMEMBER THE EVENTS OF THAT NIGHT?

AM I LATE?
I'M SORRY,
ASH.

I WILL ACCEPT THE CONSE-QUENCES.

YOU ARE... THE COLDEST MAN OF ANYONE I KNOW, ASH.

HAVE YOU EVEN THOUGHT OF PAMELA? SHE CANNOT DIE, AND SHE IS MISERABLE BECAUSE OF YOU.

PROMISE ME THAT YOU WILL KEEP THE SECRET.
A PROMISE WITH THE DEVIL...
HO, HO... YES, I PROMISE.

I'M CURIOUS ABOUT ONE THING, THOUGH: DO YOU LOVE HER?
YES, I LOVE PAMELA. BUT I LOVE MYSELF MORE.
I WANT TO ESCAPE THIS ROTTING BRIDLE CALLED IMMORTALITY-- ALIVE.
A NEW LIFE IN WHICH ONE MAY DIE, BE REBORN, AND HAVE AN END.
I LOVE PAMELA, BUT I HAVE DECIDED TO TAKE A NEW LIFE.

YOU HAVEN'T FORGOTTEN, HAVE YOU?

YOU PROBABLY DIDN'T WANT TO BE INVOLVED. YOU DIDN'T WANT TO BE MIXED UP IN THEIR FATE.
YOU HAVE PUSHED WHAT YOU HEARD INTO ONE CORNER OF YOUR MEMORY, AND YOU HAVE WATCHED LIKE A SPECTATOR UNTIL THINGS HAVE ENDED AS THEY ARE. ISN'T THAT SO?

YOUR PRIDE WAS HURT. NO MATTER HOW YOU TRIED TO IGNORE IT, THE FEELINGS ALWAYS REMAINED TO TORTURE YOU.
AND THE PEOPLE WHO CREATED YOUR SUFFERING DON'T EVEN CARE.
ISN'T THAT WHY YOU TRY TO HARBOR FEELINGS OF HATRED TOWARDS THAT WOMAN? SO THAT YOUR FEELINGS DON'T COLLAPSE INWARD?

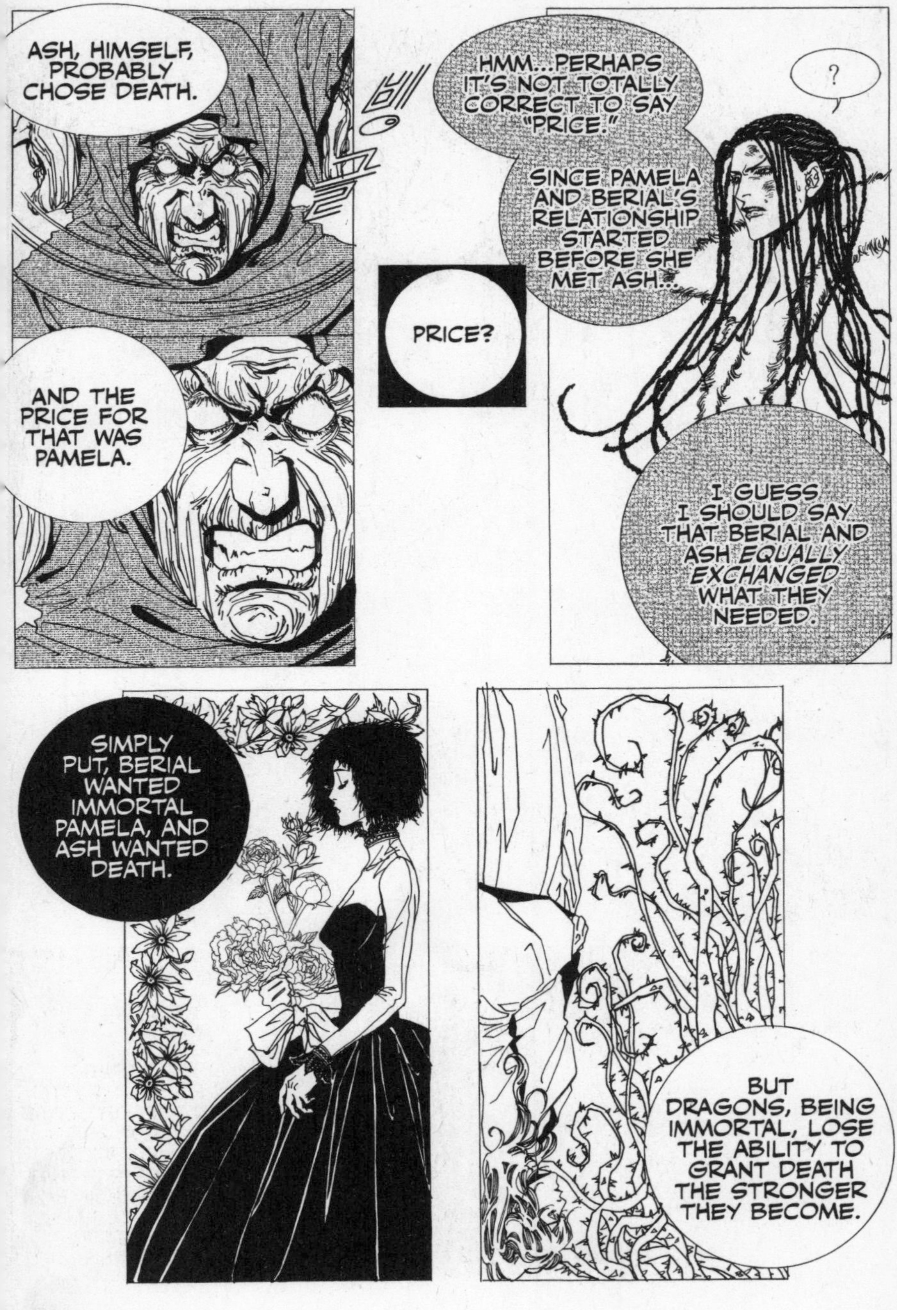

ASH, HIMSELF, PROBABLY CHOSE DEATH.

AND THE PRICE FOR THAT WAS PAMELA.

PRICE?

?

HMM...PERHAPS IT'S NOT TOTALLY CORRECT TO SAY "PRICE."

SINCE PAMELA AND BERIAL'S RELATIONSHIP STARTED BEFORE SHE MET ASH...

I GUESS I SHOULD SAY THAT BERIAL AND ASH *EQUALLY EXCHANGED* WHAT THEY NEEDED.

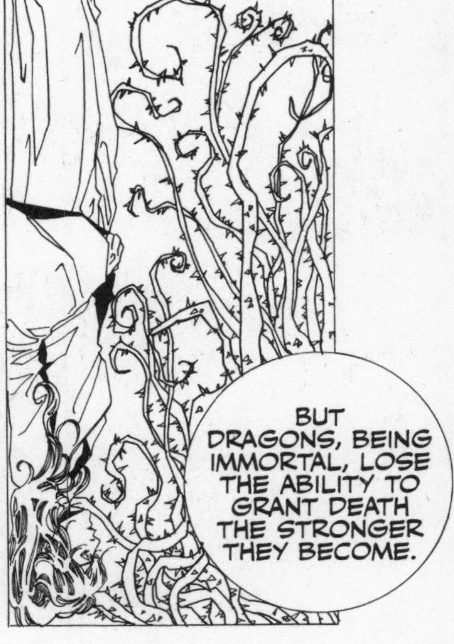

BERIAL WAS ONE OF THE FEW WHO COULD GRANT DEATH.
BERIAL MADE PAMELA IMMORTAL AND ASH WAS ABLE TO ESCAPE THAT FATE.

BERIAL AND ASH HAD THE RIGHT TIMING.

MAYBE IT'S NOT MY BUSINESS, BUT WHY BERIAL AND PAMELA...?

LITTLE CHILD! COME, HAVE SOME BREAD.

YOU'RE NO SAGE. I CAN SEE YOUR TRUE FORM, AND IT'S DIRTY, VILE AND DISTORTED.

SHE WAS ABLE TO SEE THROUGH TO THE REAL IDENTITY OF BERIAL, AND HE WAS ABLE TO RECOGNIZE HER.

EVERY-THING THAT HAPPENED STARTED THERE.

EVERYTHING WAS MEANINGLESS AND BORING FOR BERIAL UNTIL HE MET PAMELA. SHE BECAME HIS ONLY SOURCE OF ENJOYMENT.

PAMELA'S "KEEN INSIGHT," HER GIFT FROM OD, HAS BECOME THE CAUSE OF AN EXTREMELY FEARFUL WRATH.

IF THAT'S SO, OLD HAG, THEN WHY DID HE MAKE PAMELA IMMORTAL?

BERIAL IS AN IMMORTAL BEING, JUST LIKE ASH.
FOR HIM, THE HUMAN LIFE SPAN IS A MERE MOMENT.
HE WANTED TO ENJOY HER FOREVER.

I WILL TELL YOU ONE MORE THING OF INTEREST...
WHY YOU ENDED UP BEING WITH ASH...
WHO ASH IS RIGHT NOW, AND WHO *YOU* ARE... DO YOU WANT TO KNOW?
ABOUT YOU AND THE CURRENT ASH AND PAMELA...
?

HUFF
HUFF
HUFF
HUFF
I HAVE TO LET HER KNOW!
I HAVE TO TELL PAMELA THE TRUTH!

HAVE YOU BEEN
WELL, CORA?
WHERE ARE
YOU GOING IN SUCH
A HURRY?

XIII TRANSFORMATION

UKEMOCHI

MEANING OF THE CARD: Transformation. The need to allow something to die in order to create room for the new. Painful change that is necessary. Creating life out of death. Upside down, it represents fear of change. Resisting transformation.

IN MEDIEVAL TIMES...

A MONK OF THIS CHURCH, WHO COVETED POWER, ONCE SUMMONED THE DEVIL.

THIS IS MY VERY FIRST MEMORY... I CAN'T REMEMBER ANYTHING BEFORE IT.

I trust you, Cora.

I FELT SO
EMPTY BECAUSE
I COULDN'T GIVE
MY LOVE TO
ANYONE... IS THAT
WHY ASH WAS SO
IMPORTANT TO
ME?

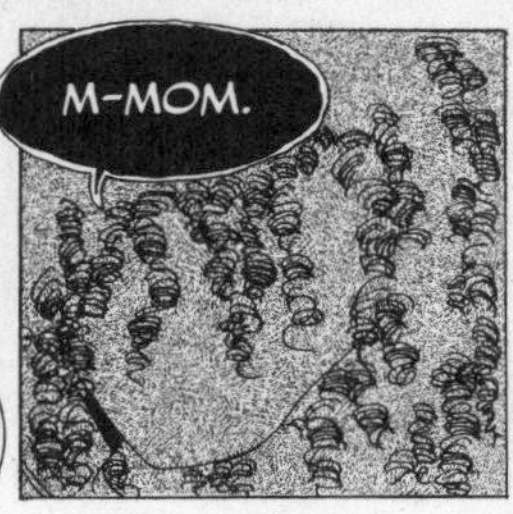

MOM...

MOM, DON'T GO. I'M AFRAID. BAD THINGS WILL HAPPEN...

DO YOU WANT TO PROTECT YOUR DAUGHTER?
ALLOW ME TO LEND YOU MY STRENGTH. ACCEPT MY OFFER, OR YOUR DAUGHTER WILL BE BURNED AS A WITCH.
ARE YOU THE DEVIL?
WHAT DOES IT MATTER?
WHAT ARE THE CONDITIONS?
I TAKE IT YOU'VE HEARD ABOUT SIGNING ONE'S LIFE AWAY TO THE DEVIL?

THANK YOU. THINGS WILL BE MUCH MORE ENTERTAINING NOW...
YOU ARE...
...THE SAGE?!!
WELL, SOME CALL ME THE "EMPEROR OF GREAT WAR," AND OTHERS REFER TO ME AS "THE ONE WHO LOVES EVIL MOST."
BUT I'M DEFINITELY NOT A SAGE. YOUR DAUGHTER WAS RIGHT.

WHAT DO YOU MEAN *DISASTROUS?* THAT'S NOT WHAT YOU PROMISED!
ALTHOUGH IT WILL BE DISASTROUS FOR PAMELA TO HAVE THE KEEN INSIGHT THAT SHE HAS.
I PROMISED THAT SHE WOULDN'T BE BURNED AT THE STAKE. I NEVER SAID I WOULDN'T TOUCH HER.
NO! LEAVE MY DAUGHTER ALONE!
I CAN'T DO THAT.

PLEASE... DON'T HARM MY DAUGHTER!

DAMN IT! I LIKED THIS BODY, AND NOW IT'S RUINED.
DID YOU REALLY THINK YOU COULD DESTROY ME THIS WAY?
A MOTHER'S LOVE IS VOID OF REASON-- IT'S PURE EMOTION.

I'LL BE SEEING YOU AGAIN...
HAH, HAH, HAH...
YAY!
HOORAY!
THE DAY IS FINALLY HERE...

...?
DON'T YOU LAY YOUR HANDS ON MY DAUGHTER!
I HOPE EVERYTHING LOOKS OKAY...
SINCE YOU DESTROYED MY BODY... I HAD TO GET A NEW ONE.
YOU'VE GOT OTHER THINGS TO WORRY ABOUT.
HAH, HAH HAH...

HAH, HAH...
HAH, HAH, HAH...
HAH, HAH, HAH...
HAH, HAH, HAH...
HAH, HAH, HAH!!

POOR THING. AT SUCH A YOUNG AGE, TOO...
I HEARD THAT SHE WAS AN ALBINO?
I HOPE SHE'S IN HEAVEN...
차아
차아

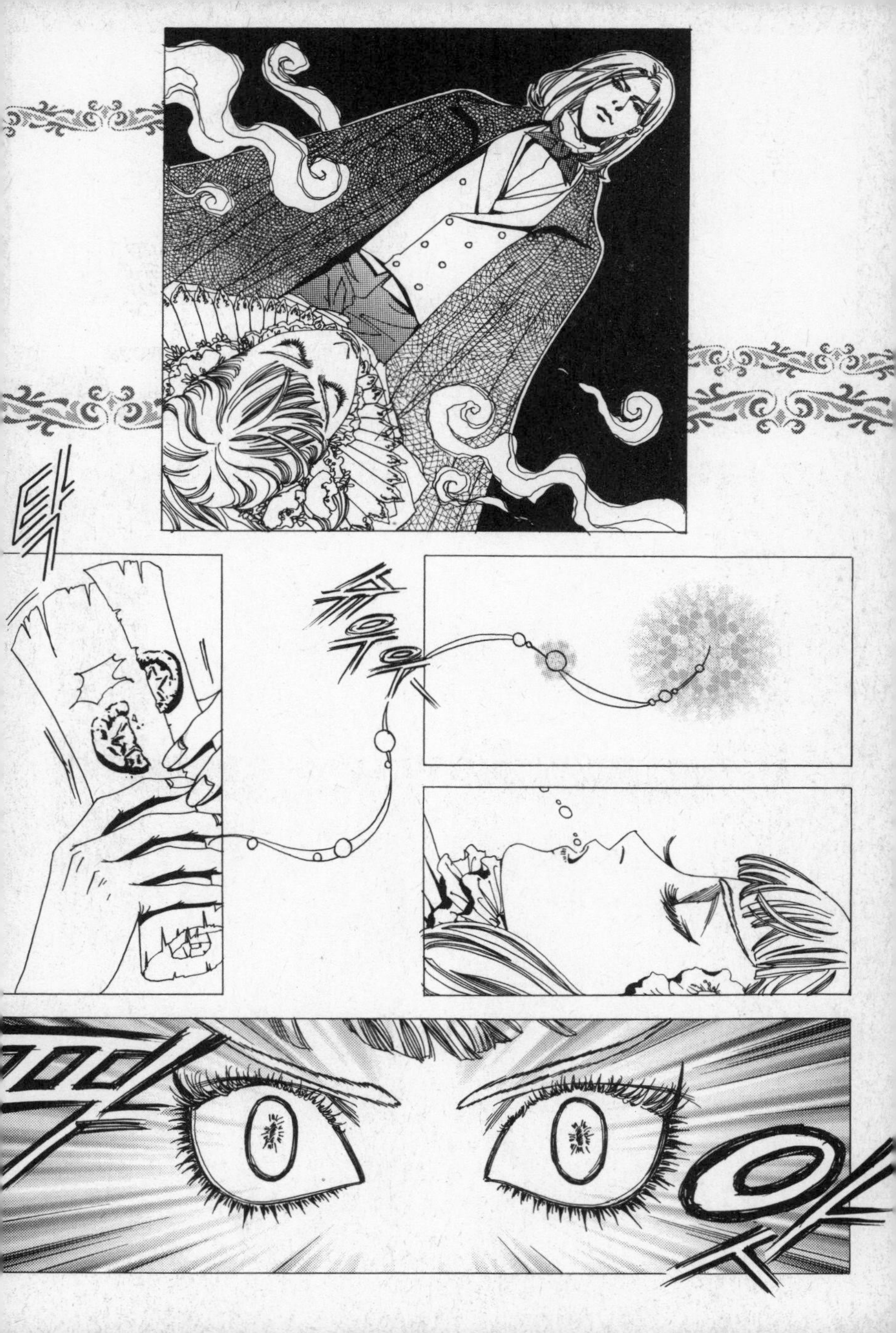
탁
슈우우
꺄아

WHERE ARE YOU GOING IN SUCH A HURRY, CORA?
I RE-MEMBER...
...WHO YOU ARE...WHO I AM...
DID ALECTO TELL YOU?
FOR SOMEONE WHO LOOKS THE QUIET TYPE, HE SURE TALKS A LOT. SO, WHAT ARE YOU GOING TO DO?

WHAT IS IT THIS TIME?

SHE WAS WORRIED BECAUSE THE SQUIRREL THAT LIVES WITH HER DISAPPEARED. I ASSURED HER HE WOULD RETURN.

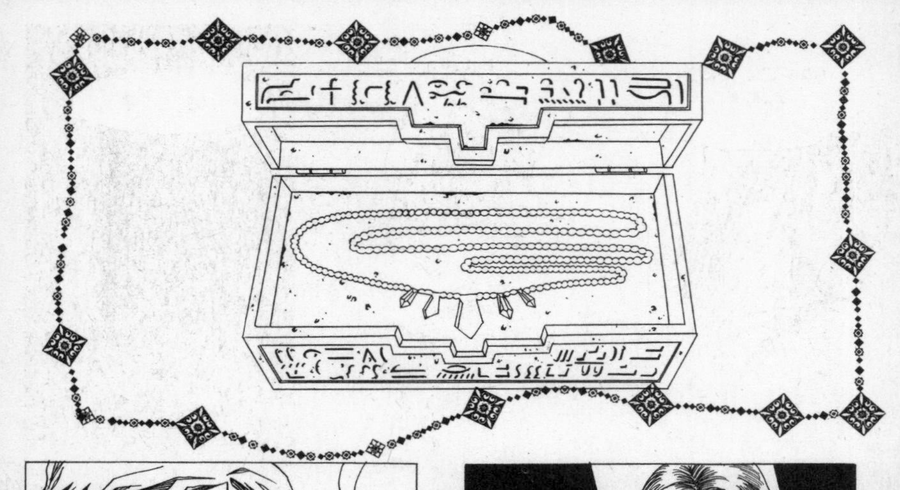

THE BOX KEEPS FILLING UP. TOO BAD...

PAMELA, GET THE PHONE.

HELLO?

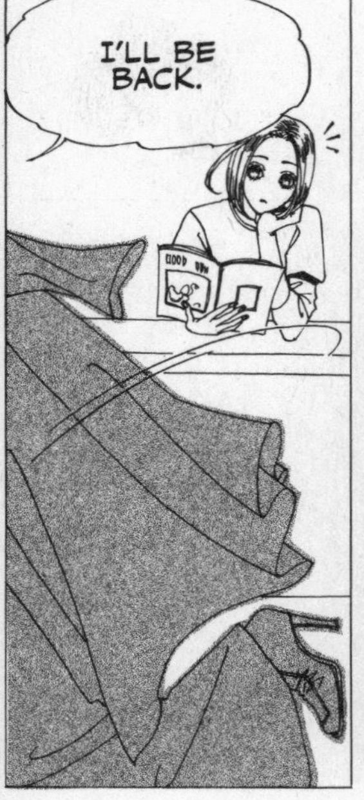

HELLO?

탁탁탁
톡
톡
THE SKY IS GREY. LOOKS LIKE IT'S GOING TO RAIN, NO?

ASH...? I THOUGHT YOU WERE HURT AND COULDN'T MOVE!
OR...
DO YOU LOVE ME, PAMELA?
SILLY WOMAN...
DO YOU BELIEVE EVERYTHING YOU HEAR?
IF...IF YOU'RE JOKING, I'M GONNA KILL YOU! I WAS WORRIED ABOUT YOU!
I HEAR THAT YOU'RE IMMORTAL.

WHAT ARE YOU TRYING TO SAY?

WHAT A PAIN. HOW AM I SUPPOSED TO DISPOSE OF YOU IF YOU CAN'T DIE?

I'M SAYING THAT I LOATHE YOU, PAMELA.

BECAUSE YOU TOOK AWAY THE MOST PRECIOUS PERSON IN MY LIFE.
I DIDN'T HAVE A NORMAL LIFE.
I DIDN'T HAVE A MOTHER OR A FATHER.
THE WAY I CAME TO EXIST IN THIS WORLD WAS DIFFERENT FROM EVERY OTHER KID...IT WAS VERY DIFFICULT FOR ME.
BAP
HELLO?

TO ME, BELUS WAS A FATHER, A FRIEND, AND A TEACHER.
I DON'T KNOW WHY HE CHOSE TO BE IN MY LIFE.
FOR AS LONG AS I CAN REMEMBER, HE HAS ALWAYS BEEN WITH ME.
HIGH SCHOOL

YOU BASTARD, WHO DO YOU THINK YOU ARE TO DEFY ME?!
YOU'RE A BASTARD--YOU HAVE NO PARENTS! THAT'S RIGHT, I CALLED YOU A BASTARD! YOU GOT A PROBLEM WITH THAT?!
YOU LITTLE BASTARD!
WHO THE HELL ARE YOU?!

IF ASH IS A BASTARD, WHAT DOES THAT MAKE YOU?
I HEARD THAT YOU WERE BORN AFTER YOUR MOM HAD AN AFFAIR WITH SOME GROCERY CLERK NAMED DAVID.
WHO THE HELL ARE YOU?!!
IF YOU THINK I'M LYING, GO HOME. SEE FOR YOUR OWN EYES WHAT YOUR MOM AND DAVID ARE UP TO!
YOU PLAN ON STAYING DOWN THERE ALL DAY?

WHEN I WAS WITH HIM, MY MIND--USUALLY WILD LIKE AN ANGRY STORM--WAS AT EASE.

BUT ONE DAY...

I THINK I HAVE TO GO BACK TO HER NOW.

THERE IS A WOMAN THAT BRINGS ME MUCH HAPPINESS.
AND I...
THAT'S WHY I HAD TO FIND YOU.
I HAD TO SEE WHAT KIND OF A WOMAN WOULD MAKE HIM THROW ME ASIDE LIKE THAT.
Good Bye
...WAS THROWN AWAY...
JUST LIKE A USED TISSUE.

ASH...?

AHH!!!

WHAT ARE YOU DOING?!! I CAN'T DIE-- NO MATTER WHAT YOU DO TO ME!

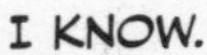

I KNOW.
THAT'S WHY I ASKED YOU TO COME HERE. LOOK DOWN.

WHAT'S THAT...?

THAT'S A DOOR THAT WAS OPENED WHEN A PRIEST ONCE SUMMONED THE DEVIL. IT HAPPENED IN THE MIDDLE AGES...
HIS SUMMONING MAGIC WASN'T PERFECT, SO EVERY 15 DAYS, THE DOOR OPENED. NOTHING'S CHANGED SINCE THEN... THIS IS THE DOOR TO HELL!!
TIME TO GO, PAMELA.
AAAH!

I FOLLOWED PAMELA BECAUSE I FELT THAT SOMETHING WAS STRANGE. APPARENTLY, YOU WERE CREATING A SCENE, ASH.
AAAH!
LET HER GO, BELUS.

STAY STRONG A BIT LONGER.
UGH!
BELUS!!

LET GO! I SAID, LET GO!!
WHY WOULD YOU GO TO SUCH LENGTHS FOR *HER?!!*
BECAUSE SHE MAKES ME HAPPIER THAN ANYONE ELSE CAN!

AAAH!!

SEVEN OF CUPS: this card stands for everything that is messy and impractical. It refers to one's over-indulgence, lack of focus and commitment, and having many options to choose from.

THE HIEROPHANT: this card is symbolic of the need to conform to previously defined rules and situations. It refers to one's pursuance of knowledge, being part of a group, and sharing a cultural heritage.

IT'S A BIT AWKWARD AROUND HERE TODAY.
IT'S LIKE TWO PEOPLE ON A BLIND DATE.
WHY ARE YOU TAKING IT OUT ON ME?!!

지글지글
치이이

ARE YOU OKAY?!! WE'D BETTER GET YOU TO THE HOSPITAL...
MY POOR PAMELA...
GO FIND ALECTO!!
HE WILL TELL YOU THE TRUTH... THE TRUTH...

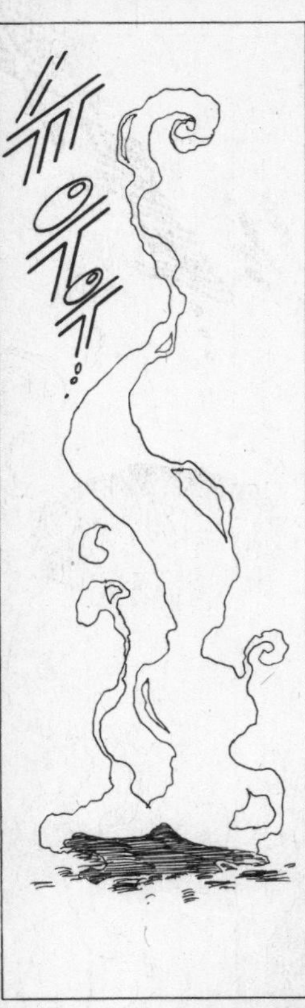

M...MOM?
털썩

SHE PASSED AWAY LONG AGO, DIDN'T SHE?

THE VOICE WAS DIFFER-ENT...
...AND SHE LOOKED DIFFER-ENT...
...BUT IT WAS CLEARLY MY MOTHER.

SOMETHING IS INSIDE THERE!!

THAT'S...
ANOTHER BEAD FROM BERIAL'S NECKLACE?!!

IN THE NEXT VOLUME OF

Tarot Café

PAMELA IS CLOSE TO COMPLETING BERIAL'S NECKLACE, BUT AT WHAT COST? AND WHAT WILL HAPPEN WHEN SHE DOES?

TORN BETWEEN HER SLOWLY RETURNING MEMORIES AND THE TRUTH BROUGHT TO HER BY HER FRIENDS, PAMELA MUST LEARN WHO IS TRULY ON HER SIDE AND WHO IS USING HER FOR THEIR OWN GAINS. AND IT MAY END UP WITH HER COMING FACE TO FACE WITH THE PERSON SHE TRUSTS THE LEAST... BERIAL.

Initial cover sketches from Sang-Sun Park for volume 1

1-2

Initial cover sketches from Sang-Sun Park for volume 2

2-2

Initial cover sketches from Sang-Sun Park for volume 3

3-2

Check out the original covers for

Tarot Café

TOKYOPOP®

The Tarot Café™

SANG-SUN PARK

TOKYOPOP

The Tarot Café™

SANG-SUN PARK

TOKYOPOP

The Tarot Café™

SANG-SUN PARK

TOKYOPOP

The Tarot Café™

SANG-SUN PARK

Also by Sang-Sun Park
Ark Angels
From a small lake nestled in a secluded forest far from the edge of town something strange emerged one day: Three sisters from another world. Equipped with their magical powers, they are charged with saving all the creatures of Earth from becoming extinct.

Chapter 1
ブワッ
ブワッ ブワッ

We come from an Earth in a parallel dimension.
Our mission is to rescue the animals of Your planet that are on the brink of extinction, preserving them in "Noah's Ark."
Our perception of Your Earth's animals is different from Yours.
We don't just see an animal's physical form, but we look inside to its soul.
That's why...we believe every life is equal and precious.

YAAAAAAA!
ドスッ!!
Our first expedition starts today.
This is Hamu. She likes to complain.
OWWWCH... YOU REALLY NEED TO WORK ON YOUR LANDINGS!
Damn! My hair is all messed up!
She is my second-oldest sister. She got the good looks, but was made disagreeable in return. She hates men with a passion.

IT'S NOT PINPIN'S FAULT. THE TURBULENCE BETWEEN DIMENSIONS MAKES IT IMPOSSIBLE TO MAINTAIN OUR FORMS.
This is my oldest sister, Shem.
She's kindhearted and is really serious about most things, but when she gets angry, she's like a monster!
HEY, CHECK IT OUT! IT LOOKS LIKE OUR CLOTHES CHANGED FOR THIS MISSION!
WELL, SINCE WE DON'T HAVE MUCH TIME...
MY name is Japheth. I'm the Youngest.
LET'S QUIT STANDING AROUND AND GET TO WORK!

ピカッ
Mariana Archipelago
Guam
THE YEAR IS 1968. THE PLACE IS GUAM'S MARIANA ARCHIPELAGO. OUR QUARRY IS THE GUAM FRUIT BAT. OUR WINDOW OF OPPORTUNITY IS 24 HOURS!

GET HIM!! IF THAT BAT GETS AWAY, NOBODY GETS PAID!! NOT FOR A WHOLE MONTH!!!
GOTCHA!!

HE'S GONE...
HUH? WHERE'D HE GO? I THOUGHT I HAD HIM...
DON'T WORRY. WE'RE NOT GOING TO EAT YOU.
WE CAME FROM ANOTHER DIMENSION TO RESCUE YOU. WE HAVE AN ARK WHERE ALL ENDANGERED SPECIES CAN LIVE FREE.
P- please, let me go...I don't want to be eaten.
I promise you, I taste terrible.
Our perception of your Earth's animals is different from yours. We don't just see an animal's physical form, but we look inside to its soul...and to us, its soul looks just like humans do.
ぶる ぶる

NOBODY KNOWS ABOUT IT, AND NOBODY WILL EVER FIND OUT, EITHER. ONCE YOU'RE ONBOARD, YOU'LL BE SAFE FOREVER.
WHEN THE EARTH BECOMES BEAUTIFUL AGAIN, WE'LL UNLOAD OUR ARK AND THE ANIMALS WILL RETURN.
BUT NOT BEFORE HUMANS LEARN TO LIVE IN HARMONY WITH THEIR ANIMAL BRETHREN.

I was the one who explained it...
I thought you were here to capture me...
CHU
...but then again, someone as beautiful as you can capture me any time she wants.
WHERE DO YOU GET OFF KISSING ME?! YOU'RE JUST A BAT!
WATCH IT, MISTER!
OOPS. HEH-HEH... ANYWAY, WE SHOULD GET OUT OF HERE.

NOT YET...WE CAN'T LEAVE YET.
Why not?
Yeah, why?
Come In
BAT
FOOT
I CAME ALL THE WAY TO GUAM BECAUSE I HEARD YOU SERVE PREMIUM FRUIT BAT CUISINE, CHEF.
UH....WELL... IF YOU COULD PLEASE BE PATIENT A LITTLE LONGER, PRESIDENT ORURUREISHON, WE HAVE THE BAT YOU DESIRE.
BUT...IT'S BEEN DAYS, AND YOU HAVEN'T SERVED A SINGLE BAT-BASED MEAL. NOT EVEN A MEASLY WING.
I KNOW IT'S GETTING LATE, SO HOW ABOUT A SIMPLE BREAKFAST TO START...?

ALL YOU'VE BEEN FEEDING ME DAY IN AND DAY OUT IS THAT SAME EXCUSE...
THAT'S A FRUIT BAT? IS IT REALLY SO TASTY? IT LOOKS CREEPY...
THAT'S YOUR MOTHER IN THE CAGE?
YES. THANK GOODNESS SHE'S STILL ALIVE.
I KNEW THIS WAS TOO EASY TO BE TRUE. SO, HOW ARE WE GOING TO SAVE HER? WE NEED A PLAN.
FROM THE SOUND OF IT, SHE'S GOING TO BE OKAY UNTIL TOMORROW MORNING. SO, WE'LL LIBERATE HER TONIGHT!
OH... TH-THANK Y--

OH, NO! NOT NOW...!
UNGHHH...I NEED TO STAY IN CONTROL...!
I CAN'T!! I CAN'T HOLD BACK ANY MORE!!

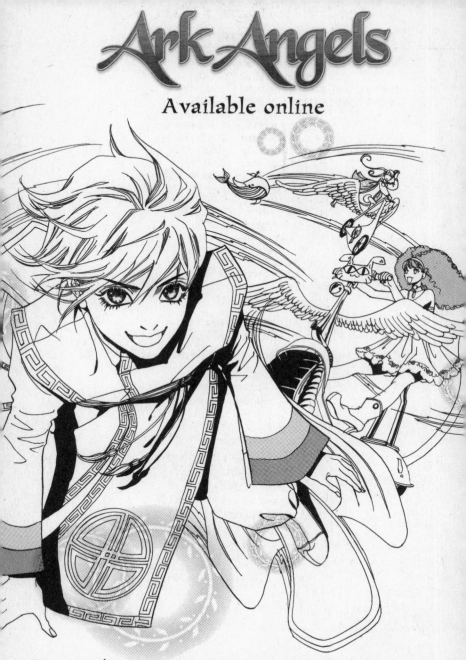